Contents

Line references in these Notes are to the
Arden Shakespeare: Richard II,
but as references are also given to particular acts
and scenes, the Notes may be used with any
edition of the play.

Preface by the general editor

The intention throughout this study aid is to stimulate and guide, to encourage your involvement in the book, and to develop informed responses and a sure understanding of the main details.

Brodie's Notes provide a clear outline of the play or novel's plot, followed by act, scene, or chapter summaries and/or commentaries. These are designed to emphasize the most important literary and factual details. Poems, stories or non-fiction texts combine brief summary with critical commentary on individual aspects or common features of the genre being examined. Textual notes define what is difficult or obscure and emphasize literary qualities. Revision questions are set at appropriate points to test your ability to appreciate the prescribed book and to write accurately and relevantly about it.

In addition, each of these Notes includes a critical appreciation of the author's art. This covers such major elements as characterization, style, structure, setting and themes. Poems are examined technically – rhyme, rhythm, for instance. In fact, any important aspect of the prescribed work will be evaluated. The aim is to send you back to the text you are studying.

Each study aid concludes with a series of general questions which require a detailed knowledge of the book: some of these questions may invite comparison with other books, some will be suitable for coursework exercises, and some could be adapted to work you are doing on another book or books. Each study aid has been adapted to meet the needs of the current examination requirements. They provide a basic, individual and imaginative response to the work being studied, and it is hoped that they will stimulate you to acquire disciplined reading habits and critical fluency.

Graham Handley 1991

Shakespeare and the Elizabethan Playhouse

William Shakespeare was born in Stratford-upon-Avon in 1564, and there are reasons to suppose that he came from a relatively prosperous family. He was probably educated at Stratford Grammar School and, at the age of eighteen, married Anne Hathaway, who was twenty-six. They had three children, a girl born shortly after their marriage, followed by twins in 1585 (the boy died in 1596). It seems likely that Shakespeare left for London shortly after a company of visiting players had visited Stratford in 1585, for by 1592 – according to the jealous testimony of one of his fellow-writers Robert Greene – he was certainly making his way both as actor and dramatist. The theatres were closed because of the plague in 1593; when they reopened Shakespeare worked with the Lord Chamberlain's men, later the King's men, and became a shareholder in each of the two theatres with which he was most closely associated, the Globe and the Blackfriars. He later purchased New Place, a considerable property in his home town of Stratford, to which he retired in 1611; there he entertained his great contemporary Ben Jonson (1572–1637) and the poet Michael Drayton (1563–1631). An astute businessman, Shakespeare lived comfortably in the town until his death in 1616.

This is a very brief outline of the life of our greatest writer, for little more can be said of him with certainty, though the plays – and poems – are living witness to the wisdom, humanity and many-faceted nature of the man. He was both popular and successful as a dramatist, perhaps less so as an actor. He probably began work as a dramatist in the late 1580s, by collaborating with other playwrights and adapting old plays, and by 1598 Francis Meres was paying tribute to his excellence in both comedy and tragedy. His first original play was probably *Love's Labour's Lost* (1590) and while the theatres were closed during the plague he wrote his narrative poems *Venus and Adonis* (1593) and *The Rape of Lucrece* (1594). The sonnets were almost certainly written in the 1590s though not published until 1609; the first 126 are addressed to a young man who was his friend and patron, while the rest are concerned with the 'dark lady'.

The dating of Shakespeare's plays has exercised scholars ever since the publication of the First Folio (1623), which listed them as comedies, histories and tragedies. It seems more important to look at them chronologically as far as possible, in order to trace Shakespeare's considerable development as a dramatist. The first period, say to the middle of the 1590s, included such plays as *Love's Labour's Lost*, *The Comedy of Errors*, *Richard III*, *The Taming of the Shrew*, *Romeo and Juliet* and *Richard II*. These early plays embrace the categories listed in the First Folio, so that Shakespeare the craftsman is evident in his capacity for variety of subject and treatment. The next phase includes *A Midsummer's Night's Dream*, *The Merchant of Venice*, *Henry IV Parts 1 and 2*, *Henry V* and *Much Ado About Nothing*, as well as *Julius Caesar*, *As You Like It* and *Twelfth Night*. These are followed, in the early years of the century, by his great tragic period: *Hamlet*, *Othello*, *King Lear* and *Macbeth*, with *Antony and Cleopatra* and *Coriolanus* belonging to 1607–09. The final phase embraces the romances (1610–13), *Cymbeline*, *The Tempest* and *The Winter's Tale* and the historical play *Henry VIII*.

Each of these revision aids will place the individual text under examination in the chronology of the remarkable dramatic output that spanned twenty years from the early 1590s to about 1613. The practical theatre for which Shakespeare wrote and acted derived from the inn courtyards in which performances had taken place, the few playhouses in his day being modelled on their structure. They were circular or hexagonal in shape, allowing the balconies and boxes around the walls full view of the stage. This large stage, which had no scenery, jutted out into the pit, the most extensive part of the theatre, where the poorer people – the 'groundlings' – stood. There was no roof (though the Blackfriars, used from 1608 onwards, was an indoor theatre) and thus bad weather meant no performance. Certain plays were acted at court, and these private performances normally marked some special occasion. Costumes, often rich ones, were used, and music was a common feature, with musicians on or under the stage; this sometimes had additional features, for example a trapdoor to facilitate the entry of a ghost. Women were barred by law from appearing on stage, and all female parts were played by boy actors; this undoubtedly explains the many instances in Shakespeare where a woman has to conceal her identity by disguising

herself as a man, e.g. Rosalind in *As You Like It*, Viola in *Twelfth Night*.

Shakespeare and his contemporaries often adapted their plays from sources in history and literature, extending an incident or a myth or creating a dramatic narrative from known facts. They were always aware of their own audiences, and frequently included topical references, sometimes of a satirical flavour, which would appeal to – and be understood by – the ground-lings as well as their wealthier patrons who occupied the boxes. Shakespeare obviously learned much from his fellow dramatists and actors, being on good terms with many of them. Ben Jonson paid generous tribute to him in the lines prefaced to the First Folio of Shakespeare's plays:

Thou art a monument without a tomb,
And art alive still, while thy book doth live
And we have wits to read, and praise to give.

Among his contemporaries were Thomas Kyd (1558–94) and Christopher Marlowe (1564–93). Kyd wrote *The Spanish Tragedy*, the revenge motif here foreshadowing the much more sophis-ticated treatment evident in *Hamlet*, while Marlowe evolved the 'mighty line' of blank verse, a combination of natural speech and elevated poetry. The quality and variety of Shakespeare's blank verse owes something to the innovatory brilliance of Marlowe but carries the stamp of individuality, richness of association, technical virtuosity and, above all, the genius of imaginative power.

The texts of Shakespeare's plays are still rich sources for scholars, and the editors of these revision aids have used the Arden editions of Shakespeare, which are regarded as pre-eminent for their scholarly approach. They are strongly recom-mended for advanced students, but other editions, like The New Penguin Shakespeare, The New Swan, The Signet are all good annotated editions currently available. A reading list of selected reliable works on the play being studied is provided at the end of each commentary and students are advised to turn to these as their interest in the play deepens.

Literary terms used in these notes

Anachronism An occurrence which takes place in an inappropriate time-setting.

Blank verse Unrhymed verse in ten-syllable lines.

Climax A crucial moment, of high emotional charge. Usually occurs just before the resolution of the drama. Increasing tension precedes climax.

Colloquial Words which are used in everyday speech.

Conceit A highly imaginative idea. A far-fetched, elaborately worked-out metaphorical comparison.

Dramatic irony Occurs when a character in a play speaks words the full significance of which he does not realize. The audience, assuming that it is in full possession of what happens in the play, *does* appreciate the full implication of the character's words.

Empathy Occurs when an audience feels that it is able to share a character's thoughts and feelings – to such an extent that it identifies completely with the character.

Imagery Any figurative use of language. Often 'word-pictures', which utilize the capacity of the mind to respond emotionally to an idea which is being evoked by the words.

Irony Occurs when the real meaning of what is expressed is at variance with what appears to be said, i.e. the surface meaning is in conflict with what is really meant.

Lyrical A highly emotional utterance, which usually betokens what is in a character's heart. Often the words have a melodious quality.

Metaphor A comparison which is unequivocally implied or expressed, without the use of 'like' or 'as'.

Pathos Occurs when a piece of writing evokes pity.

Rhetorical Language which is deliberately contrived so as to be particularly emotive or persuasive. Often associated with a publicly-delivered speech.

Rhythm Language has a natural distribution of sound-emphasis, sometimes called 'stress' or 'rhythm'. When the stresses occur regularly, it is called 'metre'.

Pun A play on words, which exploits the fact that words of the same sound may have more than one meaning.

Simile A figure of speech, introduced by 'like' or 'as', which compares two essentially dissimilar things.

Soliloquy The name given to the speech of a character in a play, when, alone on the stage, he speaks to the audience of his innermost thoughts and feelings.

Symbolism Occurs when an object has the power to evoke particular thoughts and feelings in an audience. In such instances, we can speak of an object as having particular 'associations'. Frequently something 'concrete' may symbolize something abstract, e.g. the 'crown' symbolizes kingship. Some symbols are very rich and have a host of 'associations'.

Tragedy At its simplest, a tragedy describes the 'fall' of a character. It usually describes the sufferings of this character (the 'tragic hero') and ends in his death. In Shakespeare, the fall of the character is usually attributable partly to fate and partly to some flaw in his nature.

The play

Plot

In the presence of King Richard II, Bolingbroke accuses
Thomas Mowbray of the murder of the Duke of Gloucester,
embezzlement and treason. Mowbray rejects the charges.
Richard tries to persuade the antagonists to settle their quarrel
peaceably, but his attempt fails. Matters will be settled by a
trial-at-arms.

Meanwhile, the Duchess of Gloucester seeks to persuade John
of Gaunt (Bolingbroke's father) to avenge her husband's murder by rebelling against Richard, whom she believes instigated
the deed. Gaunt refuses.

Bolingbroke and Mowbray meet at Coventry, but before the
duel can begin, Richard intervenes. He banishes Bolingbroke
for ten years – later reduced to six years; Mowbray is banished
for life.

In order to finance a military campaign in Ireland, Richard
determines to levy various illegal taxes. John of Gaunt, sensing
that his death is near, wishes to give some last-minute advice to
the irresponsible King. Richard comes to see the old man, but
refuses to give serious attention to the counsel he is offered.
Gaunt dies and Richard confiscates his estates and property,
which by right should pass down to Bolingbroke. In so doing,
the King breaks an oath which he had sworn to Bolingbroke.

Richard departs for Ireland, leaving the ageing Duke of York
in charge of the kingdom, which has been 'farmed out' to the
Earl of Wiltshire – one of the royal favourites.

Bolingbroke raises an army and, supported by Northumberland, together with others of the disaffected nobility, returns
to England to seek restoration of his inheritance. Bolingbroke's
march through England proceeds smoothly: he is popular and
has no opposition. York capitulates at Berkeley. Bolingbroke
executes three of the King's favourites at Bristol.

Returning from Ireland, Richard learns at Harlech of his
precarious situation. He meets Bolingbroke at Flint. The King
surrenders and is forced to accompany Bolingbroke to London.
In Parliament, Aumerle (York's son) is accused of the murder of
Gloucester. A bitter quarrel ensues, with many challenges
issued. Richard formally abdicates in favour of Bolingbroke,

who orders arrangements to be made for his coronation. A conspiracy is launched by Aumerle, Carlisle and the Abbot of Westminster, with a view to reinstating Richard. The King is sent to the Tower. On the way there, he meets his Queen, who has been waiting for him in the street. They take their leave, but not before they hear that there has been a change of plan: Richard is now to go to Pontefract, in Yorkshire. The Queen departs, as she must, for France.

York learns of his son's treachery towards Bolingbroke, and without hesitation determines to denounce him before the new King. Aumerle pleads for pardon, and his mother also begs that he be spared. Bolingbroke is merciful.

Sir Piers Exton, one of the King's retainers, has heard Henry calling for Richard's death – he decides to take the matter in hand. Richard is murdered by Exton at Pontefract.

When the King is presented with Richard's body, he is not grateful to Exton. Weighed down by guilt, Bolingbroke proposes to go on a Crusade to atone for Richard's death. The play ends on a note of mourning.

Date

Richard II was first published, anonymously, in 1597. A year later, another edition appeared, this time bearing Shakespeare's name. Both these editions omitted the Deposition Scene, presumably because of the sensitivities of Elizabeth I, who was old and childless. There was a grave question-mark over the succession. A full version of the play appeared in 1608, when such sensitivities were no longer of relevance. All three of these editions were in Quarto. The first Folio edition appeared in 1623.

Sources and their treatment

Shakespeare's main source for this play was Holinshed's *Chronicles of England, Scotland and Ireland*, published in 1577. As usual, however, he adapted his source-material as he felt necessary, and invented scenes – all in furthering his dramatic purposes. It will be useful to consider a few examples.

(a) Holinshed deals with the course of Richard's Irish campaign. It is omitted by Shakespeare. The reason here is obviously dictated by the dramatist's need to concentrate the action of the play on the conflict between Richard and Bolingbroke. A detailed enactment of the campaign would be a distraction.

(b) Holinshed relates that Richard was ambushed by Northumberland and brought before Bolingbroke at Flint Castle. Shakespeare simply makes them meet at Flint; thus Bolingbroke is relieved of the odium of deviousness.

(c) Gaunt's character in Holinshed is unsympathetic. Shakespeare makes Gaunt a sympathetic and authoritative figure. It is dramatically useful that the audience should see him as a reliable commentator on the follies of Richard. Also, Richard's mockery and frivolous behaviour in front of this good old man, establishes the King's irresponsibility in vivid dramatic terms.

(d) Shakespeare invents the scenes in which the Queen grieves and parts from her husband. The Queen is thus used to heighten our sympathies for Richard and condition us to feel the pathos of his situation.

(e) The 'Garden Scene' is pure invention. It provides a glimpse of ordinary people, and, more importantly, forms a reliable commentary, from a disinterested source, on the action of the play and the state of England.

Other minor sources of the play are: Marlowe's *Edward II*, which also deals with a deposition; Daniel's *The Civil Wars between Lancaster and York*, which mentions the relationship between Richard and his Queen. There is a faint possibility that Froissart's *Chronicles* may have suggested the character of Gaunt as Shakespeare portrays him, but this is hypothetical. It is much more likely, as we have said, that Gaunt is Shakespeare's own invention.

Finally, the serious student may find interesting A. P. Rossiter's discussion of the influence of *Woodstock* – an anonymous play which deals with Gloucester's murder. Details of this possible source-material, and its bearing on Richard II, are to be found in *Angel with Horns* (see *Further Reading*).

Setting

The play deals with the last two years of Richard's reign. Shakespeare is not concerned to give the play a 'period' flavour – it would have been acted in the dress of his day, and such references to local colour as we find relate to Elizabethan times rather than the late 14th century. Hence, the well-known, anachronistic references to hawking (I,1,109), bear-baiting (IV,1,238), bowls (III,4,3-5) – all pastimes which would have been familiar to Elizabethans. In this context, we may also note that Richard's reference to a clock (V,5,50–58) evidently refers to an Elizabethan time-piece.

The Tournament Scene (I,3), however, does have a medieval ambience.

Scene summaries, critical commentary, textual notes and revision questions

Act I Scene 1

The scene opens on a note of discord: in the presence of Richard, Bolingbroke, attended by his father John of Gaunt, accuses Thomas Mowbray of treason – a charge which is vehemently denied. Bolingbroke proceeds to challenge Mowbray to single combat – a challenge which is accepted. Throughout these exchanges, Richard listens to the protagonists. Bolingbroke lays some specific charges against Mowbray: that he has appropriated money which was due to the King, that he has plotted treason and that he murdered the Duke of Gloucester, the King's uncle, whilst he held him for 'safe-keeping', in his castle at Calais. Mowbray denies embezzlement, murder and treason, but he admits that he had once contrived against the life of John of Gaunt (Lancaster), for which offence he has confessed to the King and has manifested repentance.

Richard attempts to calm the anger of Bolingbroke and Mowbray, but to no avail, and eventually agrees to a trial by combat at Coventry on St Lambert's Day. The Lord Marshal is ordered to make appropriate arrangements.

Commentary

The stormy opening to this scene reflects the troubled kingdom. Richard with fine words attempts to pacify Bolingbroke and Mowbray, but significantly his pleas to 'Forget, forgive' fall upon deaf ears. His statement 'We were not born to sue, but to command' has an ironic ring in the light of future events.

It is important to bear in mind that Richard was responsible for the death of Gloucester, and thus Bolingbroke's denunciation of Mowbray is a direct challenge to the King. Mowbray, in refusing to reveal that it was Richard who was behind the killing, to some extent earns our sympathy. But his disavowal of responsibility is little more than bluster, and Bolingbroke's words carry noticeably more force. It may also be remarked that Richard is apparently willing to sacrifice the honour of his agent in the interests of a patched-up peace. Thus, for all his apparent kingliness of bearing and utterance in this scene, Richard is acting from a position of weakness.

In a dramatic sense, Shakespeare opens the play in an arresting fashion: the audience finds itself caught up in a violent quarrel. Also, the political and personal strength of Bolingbroke is immediately established, as well as the real insecurity of the King.

There is also an underlying suggestion of one of the central issues of the play: the King rules by Divine Right and clearly sees himself as the 'physician', whose appointed function is to heal the wound in his kingdom, and failing this, to see that justice is done through the trial of combat at Coventry. In his role as healer and justicer he may be considered to be 'God's deputy' on earth. Bolingbroke and Mowbray both pay lip-service to the loyalty that they owe to the King. But the problem arises, in this scene and in the play as a whole, when the rightful monarch has to contend with a subject (Bolingbroke), who is evidently possessed of qualities which fit him for rule in more abundance than the King himself.

It may be significant that, at one point in the scene, Richard pointedly remarks that were Bolingbroke 'my brother, nay, our kingdom's heir,/ As he is but my father's brother's son' he could expect no privileges, when it comes to the impartial justice of a king. This apparently casual reference to Bolingbroke may indicate that Richard sees him as a rival to the throne.

band Bond.
boist'rous Clamorous, violently fierce.
late appeal Recent accusation, indictment. An appeal was a formal challenge, which denoted that the appellant was prepared to prove by single combat the truth of what he alleged.
High-stomach'd Haughty.
hap Fortune.
an immortal title i.e. crown you with immortality.
object The charge.
Tend'ring Holding dear.
misbegotten Ill-conceived, with malicious intent.
appellant As an accuser.
miscreant Villain.
Too good . . . to live i.e. too high-ranking to besmirch yourself with treachery and therefore too wicked to be allowed to live.
aggravate the note Make the disgrace the worse.
right drawn i.e. drawn in a rightful cause.
trial . . . war i.e. Mowbray does not want the matter settled in a female fashion, to be a mere war of words.
cool'd i.e. by being shed.
fair reverence Worthy respect.

post Travel with the utmost speed.

royalty Bolingbroke was the King's first cousin.

allow him odds Allow him to have an advantage over me.

were I . . . Alps Even if I were obliged to run against him in a race which demanded that I run as far as the Alps.

durst Dares.

throw my gage A glove was thrown down as an indication of a challenge. Cf. 'throwing down the gauntlet'.

pawn Pledge.

rites of knighthood Customs of chivalry.

or . . . devise Or any worse charges that you can fabricate against me.

in any fair degree In any appropriate and honourable manner.

light Alight.

nobles Gold coins.

lendings Money paid in advance of full payment.

lewd Base.

injurious Wicked.

eighteen years i.e. since the rebellion of Wat Tyler (1381).

Fetch Originate.

head and spring Source and inspiration.

Duke of Gloucester Thomas Woodstock, youngest of Edward III sons. He died in Mowbray's castle in Calais; allegedly, Richard 'inspired' his death.

Suggest Incite, instigate.

To me In taking upon himself the vengeance for Gloucester's death, Bolingbroke is probably making a scarcely veiled threat to the King.

pitch A term derived from falconry: the highest point to which the bird might soar. The King's remark here may well indicate that he feels threatened by Bolingbroke.

my kingdom's heir Dramatic irony. Little does Richard know that Bolingbroke is to succeed him, although he is not his heir.

sceptre's awe The reverence due to the sceptre (symbol of kingly authority).

partialize Make partial.

as low . . . throat You lie in your throat, even to the very depths of your heart.

receipt The money I received.

Callice Calais.

Upon . . . dear account As the balance for a heavy debt.

Neglected my sworn duty Ambiguous: according to Holinshed, Mowbray delayed in carrying out Gloucester's murder, despite the fac that he had been ordered to do so by Richard. Bolingbroke would see it differently: in permitting the murder of Gloucester, Mowbray had neglected the assurance he gave that he would give Gloucester *safe-*keeping.

Which i.e. which accusations . . .

interchangeably In reply.

overweening Presumptuous.

best blood Heart's-blood which is housed in his bosom.

choler Anger.

Our doctors . . . bleed According to the medical belief of the time, treatment of a patient (in this case blood-letting) was more likely to be successful if undertaken during particular months. Relevant calculations depended upon the astrological details of the patient, the disease and the remedy.

no boot No help for it – but to obey.

My life . . . not have Mowbray implies that the King may command his loyalty and duty unto death, but he will not surrender his honour which survives him after death.

impeach'd Accused of treason.

baffl'd A 'technical' word which refers to being disgraced as a knight.

lions make leopards tame The King's coat-of-arms was three lions; Mowbray's was a leopard.

mortal times Life on earth.

loam Mud.

impeach my height Discredit my high birth.

out-dar'd dastard This coward which I have excelled in daring.

feeble wrong Such a feebly-presented wrong.

parle Parley. An offer of peace before battle.

motive i.e. the tongue, the means by which fear is expressed.

Saint Lambert's day 17 September.

atone Make you one.

design . . . chivalry Let the result of the contest indicate who is the true knight.

Act I Scene 2

The distraught widow of the Duke of Gloucester pleads with John of Gaunt to avenge the death of her husband but he will not lift up his hand against the anointed monarch. The Duchess bids farewell to Gaunt, who is going to Coventry, and expresses the hope that Mowbray will fall at the hands of Bolingbroke (Hereford).

Commentary

This scene forms a bridge between the challenge scene which preceded it, and the confrontation at Coventry which is to follow. After the formality of council chamber, the grief of the Duchess strikes a much more personal note and we learn of the involvement of Richard in the murder of Gloucester. In her attempt to stir Gaunt to vengeance she fails, despite her reminder that Gaunt has lost a brother and may well find his own life threatened by his inaction. Gaunt's refusal to act owes its origin to a belief in the 'divinity that doth hedge a king': Richard rules by Divine Right, he is 'God's substitute' and thus to threaten him is to commit an act of sacrilege. This throws into relief the later actions of Bolingbroke, who is not restrained by such considerations. Gaunt's only comfort is to suggest that vengeance be left to God, whose aid may be sought by means of prayer.

In emphasizing the blood on the hands of Richard, the scene tends to diminish the kingly impression of him which we received in the first scene: it is no longer possible to see him as the impartial dispenser of justice, and clearly he is deeply-implicated in foul deeds.

Woodstock Thomas Woodstock, Duke of Gloucester. Son of Edward III, brother of John of Gaunt, Duke of Lancaster.

solicit Prompt.

But . . . cannot correct Punishment for the death of Gloucester is the prerogative of the King, but the King is the offender and thus 'correction' of the offence must be put in the hands of God. Gaunt states that it is not his function to take action against the King.

dried by nature's course i.e. 'withered', grown old.

by the Destinies cut Died before their natural span had expired. Applies particularly to Edward, the Black Prince – father of Richard.

mettle Spirit.

that self mould The image obviously derives from the casting of metal. Lancaster is reminded that his 'casting' is from the same 'mould' as Gloucester – and both were derived from the illustrious Edward III. The Duchess, in this sense, sees the death of her husband as an outrage against Lancaster.

model The Duchess sees Gloucester as a 'model' of Edward III and thus implies that, in ignoring the death of her husband, Gaunt is, in effect, winking at the murder of his father.

naked pathway to thy life It is suggested that by taking no action against the murderers, Gaunt is opening the way to attempts upon his own life.

mean Common.

God's substitute . . . i.e. The King.

Cousin Relative.

fell Savage.

career Charge (in the combat).

courser Horse.

lists The space set aside for a tournament to take place.

caitive recreant A captive coward.

boundeth Rebounds. The Duchess cannot prevent her grief from recurring, like a bouncing ball.

Plashy The residence of the Duke of Gloucester. Felsted, Essex.

unfurnish'd Without tapestry wall-coverings. A sign that a family was no longer in residence.

offices Servants' quarters.

Act I Scene 3

Amidst much chivalric pomp and pageantry, the combatants prepare for the trial by combat. The King presides and the Council is in attendance. Mowbray and Bolingbroke, in accordance with 'the rules', introduce themselves and state their quarrel yet again. Formal farewells are spoken and heralds identify and pronounce the readiness of the 'champions'. The charge is sounded.

Suddenly, the King throws down his 'warder', thus calling a halt to the tournament. He conducts a brief Council meeting, from which it emerges that he has decided to sentence Bolingbroke and Norfolk to banishment: the former for ten years, the latter for life.

Norfolk bewails the severity of the sentence. Richard extracts an oath from the rivals that they will adhere to the terms which he has imposed, and that they will not communicate with each other, nor effect any kind of reconciliation so that they may conspire against him.

In response to the pleading of John of Gaunt, Bolingbroke's sentence is commuted to six years banishment, but no such clemency is granted to Norfolk. The King leaves the scene.

Finally, John of Gaunt attempts to console his son: but his efforts fall upon deaf ears. Bolingbroke bids farewell to his father, stating that although he may be banished he is still 'a true-born Englishman'.

Commentary

The scene opens on a note of high pageantry. The bitterness and hostility of the two protagonists is disciplined by the demands of the rules of combat. Formal speeches are made: the language is stiff and rhetorical. Clearly Richard's love of spectacle would be well-satisfied with the proceedings, especially as he, in effect, is the person who commands centre stage – in the midst of his assembled courtiers.

But the orderly flow of events is interrupted by the King throwing down his mace. Obviously this 'surprise' represents the central dramatic moment of the scene.

Richard's decision to banish Norfolk and Bolingbroke has been variously interpreted. Some critics maintain that it is an example of the King's capricious whim. It can also be seen as a shrewd political move in which he gets rid of two potential threats to his throne. In this case, the theory would be that if one of the duellists survived, then his status might be enhanced, and thus he might be the more to be feared. As we have seen, it would not be in Richard's interests for Mowbray to win – for he knows of the King's involvement in the death of Gloucester; Bolingbroke is self-evidently ambitious. The trial-at-arms also gives the King the appearance of being in control of events.

Richard's decision to banish Mowbray for life, whereas he dismisses Bolingbroke for a mere ten years, again might be interpreted as mere whim. Arguably, however, it may reflect the greater popularity of Bolingbroke. In any case, the King makes it appear that he reduces the sentence out of pity for the ancient John of Gaunt.

Once again, if one reflects on the scene as a whole, the appearance is given that the King is fully in control, and indeed, all the major characters pronounce their loyalty to him. But this is a public moment and one could hardly expect otherwise. Nonetheless, there is much talk of treachery (notably from Norfolk and Bolingbroke) and this creates the impression of a very troubled realm. Richard, too, it might be said, does not appear to be in proper control. There is some truth in the contention that he speaks nobly, but acts weakly. He failed to reconcile the antagonists in Scene 1 and was eventually forced to accede to their wishes for a trial-at-arms. He sets this in motion, then stops it. He changes his mind over the terms of banishment – policy maybe – but hardly does it give an impression of strength and consistency. Although we have not really had time to get to grips with Richard as a character, the suspicion is not far away that he may be a deeply-flawed man.

Aumerle Son of the Duke of York.

sprightfully Full of spirit.

orderly According to the customary manner.

defend Forbid.

my succeeding issue Norfolk is defending his successors from the taint of treachery. The implication is that succeeding generations of the Norfolk family would always bear the stigma of 'traitor'.

Depose him Examine him under oath.

daring-hardy A compound adjective meaning 'bold to the point of folly'.

designs Undertakings.

vow . . . pilgrimage A vow to undertake a pilgrimage was customary in order to avert some crisis – in the hope that the wrath of God might be averted. It has a strongly ironical ring here, in view of the fact that the 'pilgrimage' which Bolingbroke is shortly to undertake will lead him to the throne.

my blood My kinsman.

profane a tear Bolingbroke implies that if anyone sheds a tear at his death in this conflict then it will be for the death of a traitor and thus 'unsanctified' weeping. Believing in the justice of his cause, he does not really believe that he is about to be killed, of course. This is merely a rhetorical flourish.

lusty Full of youthful high spirits.

English feasts Traditionally feasts ended with the daintiest morsels – sweetmeats.

regreet Greet again.

O thou i.e. John of Gaunt.

regenerate Reborn.

proof Gaunt's prayers will make the armour proof against all onslaughts.

waxen i.e. as if it were composed of wax.

furbish Make as new. The implication is that the honour of Gaunt had grown somewhat tarnished.

amazing Stupefying.

casque Helmet.

pernicious Destructive, fatal.

golden Precious.

jocund Merry.

to jest i.e. as if to a mock-combat.

approve Prove

warder A mace, or staff of office, which belonged to one presiding over a tournament. To throw it down indicated that the fighting was to stop.

aspect Sight.

civil wounds Wounds received in civil war. Ironical that Richard should wish this, of course.

eagle-winged The eagle was a symbol of royalty, and linked with the 'sky-ambitious' thoughts later in the sentence, may well indicate that Richard feels himself threatened.

Sweet infant Infant because peace has only existed for a short time.

dearer merit More valuable reward.

in the common air To consort with common people.

viol A stringed instrument, similar to the modern viola.

cunning Skilfully made, or an instrument that requires a skilful player.

being open i.e. not in its case.

portcullis'd A portcullis was a heavy gate which could be lowered to protect the entrance to a castle.

boots Profits.

compassionate Self-pitying.

plaining Lamenting.

Return again The King speaks to Norfolk.

therein i.e. in your duty.

Embrace . . . love Richard seeks to avoid Bolingbroke and Norfolk forming an alliance against him.

This louring tempest This storm of hatred.

home-bred Fostered between you at home.

advised Deliberate.

so far . . . enemy The oath is not broken: Bolingbroke has just sworn never to speak to Norfolk *as a friend*.

blotted from the book of life A reference to *Revelation*, 3,5: 'He that overcometh, shall be thus clothed in white array, and I will not blot out his name out of the booke of life.'

shall rue Learn to his regret.

stray Go astray.

glasses Gaunt's eyes are likened to looking-glasses – he is weeping.

wanton Luxuriant.

bring . . . about Change their seasons.

furrow Wrinkle.

current Valid.

party-verdict gave Implies that Gaunt, as a member of the Council, was a party to the decision to banish his own son.

lour Look with ill-favour towards.

Things . . . sour Gaunt says that he did not realize, when he acted as a judge, what the implication of his son's sentence would be. He did not envisage the effect on him as a father.

to smooth . . . mild I should have been the more ready to gloss over his faults.

partial slander The accusation that I was being biased.

I look'd when I waited for

I was . . way I was acting too strictly in approving my son's banishment.

what presence . . . know What I cannot learn from you in person.

let paper i.e. write to me.

prodigal Lavish.

to breathe To express.

dolour Grief.

sullen passage . . . return Gaunt tells Bolingbroke to contrast the sadness of his exile with the joy of his return.

jewels That which is most valuable to him in life, which can only be found in England.

Must I not . . . grief An elaborately worked-out metaphor. He implies that his exile is like a long and burdensome apprenticeship, which will terminate in no further gain of knowledge than the awareness that he has served a long and burdensome apprenticeship!

eye of heaven The sun.

virtue Power.

purchase Gain.

Look Pretend.

measure Dance.

gnarling Snarling.

sets it light Considers it of little value.

Caucasus Refers to the mountains of southern Russia.

cloy Satisfy.

fantastic Imaginary.

apprehension Conception.

Gives . . . the worse To conceive of good things only makes us the more keenly aware of the worst aspects of our present situation.

Fell . . . sore The general sense of these lines depends upon our seeing the pain of sorrow as resembling the bite of a dog. This sort of bite produces festering wounds and in this respect does not resemble the surgeon's lance-wound, which has a curative effect on the sufferer. The implication is that the feeble platitudes of Gaunt only make matters worse, whereas the clean, deep incision of the truth about his situation, would be more likely to help him to come to terms with it.

bring Accompany.

that bears me yet On which I still stand.

Act I Scene 4

Aumerle describes, in mocking tones, the departure of Boling-broke into exile. Richard revels in the description and in this scene we observe him in the midst of his favourites. The King also reveals his true motives for dispatching Bolingbroke: he resented his growing popularity with the people. Next, Richard turns his attention to a forthcoming campaign in Ireland. He intends that it be undertaken immediately and proposes to finance it by dubious means: he will raise money by handing over revenues in return for a fixed sum – to be paid now; he will force rich men to write blank cheques, to be filled in at the discretion of the Crown; and, furthermore, he is prepared simply to confiscate the estates of John of Gaunt, when he dies. On hearing that Gaunt has been taken ill, he proposes to visit him – at the same time praying that he may arrive only to hear of his death.

Commentary

Here, surrounded by his favourites, Richard reveals the unattractive side of his nature and alienates our sympathies. His levity at the banishment of Bolingbroke, his contempt for the common people, his spendthrift and dishonest means of raising money – all mark him down as a bad king.

The contrast with his conduct at Coventry is noteworthy, and Shakespeare has clearly juxtaposed this scene to make the point that the King has two faces: one for public consumption, another for his private moments. Fine and noble words in public now give way to sneers and jibes – even directed towards the old and dying Gaunt. In the interests of raising some quick money, for a dubious military enterprise, Richard is almost prepared to 'farm' out England – in abrogation of the responsibilities of a monarch. He is not above simple extortion and robbery.

Whilst the King's words of Bolingbroke, spoken in contempt, seem merely to reflect aristocratic and unthinking disdain of the masses, they also serve to heighten Bolingbroke, who clearly shows a perception of where power may lie. They also reveal a shrewd understanding of crowd sympathies. Yet, so far, all we have seen of Bolingbroke has shown a clarity of purpose and dignity. The King regards him as a threat; in the meantime, whilst he pursues a campaign in Ireland, 'God's substitute' is seen to be prepared to hand over his authority to his own dishonourable 'substitutes'.

high Proud.
highway Aumerle's levity, in punning here, is distasteful.
rheum Moisture.
hollow Insincere.
To counterfeit . . . grave. To pretend such grief possessed me that I could not speak for sorrow.
craftsmen . . . craft A pun: Bolingbroke used 'craft' (cunning) to seduce craftsmen to his side.
underbearing Endurance.
his fortune i.e. misfortune.
As 'twere . . . him As if he were attempting to carry off into banishment with him his admirer's affections. Richard believes that such affections rightly belong to him.
tribute . . . knee Bolingbroke bowed the knee to his admirers.
As were . . . in hope As if England, now in my possession, was bound on my death to revert to him, and he were the next king which my subjects had to hope for.
Expedient manage Urgent measures must be taken.
largess Gifts.
farm Lease out.
blank charters In effect, blank cheques which could be filled in according to the sum required.
subscribe The amount will be inserted on the blank charters.
presently At once.
taken Taken ill.

Revision questions on Act I

1 Outline the kingly qualities which Richard displays in Scene 1.

2 What contribution to our understanding of the King is made by the Duchess of Gloucester?

3 Give possible reasons for a) Richard deciding to halt the trial by combat and impose banishment on Bolingbroke and Mowbray, b) the difference between the respective lengths of exile, and c) the further lessening of Bolingbroke's sentence from ten to six years.

4 Discuss the presentation of Richard in the final scene of the Act.

5 What estimate do you form of the character of John of Gaunt in Act I, and what dramatic function do you think he fulfils?

6 What do we learn in Act I of Bolingbroke's character? Do you find that Shakespeare differentiates him from Mowbray?

7 Discuss the juxtaposition of scenes in this act, with particular reference to the variety of mood and atmosphere.

Act II Scene 1

John of Gaunt, nearing death, hopes that his 'wholesome counsel' will command the attention of the King. York doubts that Richard will listen, because he is given over to a life dominated by flattery and self-indulgence. Prophetically, Gaunt sees the ultimate self-destruction of the King, and then goes on to lament the fate of England, which has been, in effect, pillaged by a spendthrift and irresponsible monarch.

It is clear, from the moment that the King arrives, that he is not prepared to heed good advice: his attitude is careless and sneering, although it would appear that what he hears brings a pallor to his cheeks. York, although he agrees with the admonitions of his brother, attempts to smooth the King's ruffled feathers, as Gaunt is conveyed to his death-bed.

When he hears of the death of Gaunt from Northumberland, the King manifests no sorrow, but, after a perfunctory remark, proceeds to talk of his forthcoming Irish campaign. At this insensitivity, even York is moved to speak strong words of rebuke to his King, but they fall upon deaf ears. York has been particularly outraged by Richard's expressed intention to seize upon 'the plate, coin, revenues, and moveables' of the dead Gaunt – thus disinheriting Bolingbroke. Again, despite the manifest folly and wickedness of this action, Richard is unmoved. The Earl of Wiltshire is to be given the responsibility of overseeing the confiscation.

Ross, Willoughby and Northumberland, after ascertaining

their mutual hatred of the King, next discuss the possibility of rebellion. At first, their conversation is guarded, but they come out into the open when Northumberland reveals that Bolingbroke has already broken the terms of his exile, and is sailing towards Ravenspurgh – at the head of a considerable force of arms. The scene ends on a note of urgency as Ross, Willoughby and Northumberland hasten away to join the Bolingbroke faction.

Commentary

The opening sequence of this scene emphasizes, should we be in any doubt, the total unfitness of Richard to rule over England. His dismissive levity in the presence of the dying Gaunt, shockingly contrasts with the solemnity of the warnings which are given to him. Gaunt's patriotic lament over the England which Richard has betrayed has become justly famous. This speech, formal and rhetorical, evokes the unique preciousness and beauty of the land, which the King is prepared to mortgage out in grubby deals.

Gaunt's speech is strategically placed and its quasi-religious tone is significant. In a sense, it defines Richard as the bad ruler of a 'sacred' land ('this blessed plot'). The difficulty arises because Richard, bad king though he may be, reigns by divine sanction – he is 'God's substitute', the anointed monarch. It is not long before we hear of the arrival of Bolingbroke, who possesses strength of character, political know-how and mass-appeal – all necessary qualities of kingship. The stumbling-block is that, to become king, he must usurp the throne from God's appointed monarch and this, at best, can only be a temporary 'solution' to England's needs. John of Gaunt's sanctified England can only become a reality when the rightful king reigns over the kingdom, and this must await the arrival of the Tudor dynasty. Significantly Gaunt does not propose rebellion as a solution to the problem.

Richard's confiscation of Gaunt's lands is also an important moment and brings into focus York, who rebukes him roundly – stressing the illegality of the action. York speaks with the authority of the last of Edward's sons: he foresees that the King will bring upon himself dire consequences. York also indicates that in seizing the inheritance of Bolingbroke, the King violates the God-given laws of succession and thus forfeits his right to depend upon them when the time comes.

As the King departs on a fruitless campaign, so the stage is left empty for Bolingbroke to occupy.

unstaid Uncontrolled.
Inforce Demand.
glose Flatter.
music at close i.e. the dying cadence of a piece of music.
As . . . last As the last taste of sweets, are at their sweetest at the moment before they pass away.
Writ . . . long past Stay fresh in the memory, more so than things uttered long ago.
sad tale Serious message.
fashions in proud Italy An allusion to the tendency of the English to ape Italian fashions in dress – and other 'decadent' Italian ways.
tardy-apish Given to imitate the ways of others ('tardy' because the imitation was late in being achieved).
So So long as it is (new).
there's no respect i.e. it is immaterial
will Wilfulness rebels against what common sense holds to be proper.
breath . . . breath A pun: you haven't much breath left, so you shouldn't waste it on him.
betimes Quickly, soon.
cormorant A bird well-known for gulping its food, with apparent gluttony.
means Its resources of food.
earth of majesty i.e. the proper home of majesty.
Fear'd by their breed Whose breeding (in England) made them to be feared (by lesser breeds).
the sepulchre in stubborn Jewry A reference to the Crusades which were undertaken to regain possession of the tomb of Christ in Palestine. The Jews are stubborn because of their refusal to accept Christ as the Messaiah.
tenement Land held by a tenant.
pelting Paltry.
bound in with shame In shameful bondage.
inky blots . . . bonds The idea is that England is subject to the ill-written, corrupt legal documents with which the realm has been leased out, so that Richard may raise money to finance his extravagances.
What comfort, man? Richard's tone is insensitively frivolous.
composition Constitution.
Gaunt This word-play is either inappropriately tedious and unlikely or it may indicate that Gaunt's anger is seeking an outlet in this self-derogatory series of puns – he distracts himself from an outburst.
Watching Lying awake.
strict fast The implication is that Gaunt has been denied the 'food' which normally nourishes fathers – the company of their sons.
inherits Possesses.

nicely In such a foolishly precise way.

misery ... itself It is the sport of misery to indulge in self-mockery.

to kill my name Gaunt may have some inkling that Richard intends to disinherit Bolingbroke, thus obliterating the family title. At any rate, the King has besmirched the family honour (name) by his treatment of Bolingbroke.

I see ... seeing ill There are several plays on 'ill' here. 'I see thee ill' – I can't see you clearly and I see that you are morally sick. 'I'll in myself to see' – For because I am sick I cannot see you clearly. 'Seeing ill' – but I can certainly see evil in you. Thus: 'I am sick, but I see you for what you are – and what I see makes me ill, for I see a great deal of ill in you.'!

Thy death-bed ... thee i.e. Richard has made his kingdom his own death-bed (a prophetic utterance), and like a thoughtless patient, who does not recognize that he is sick, he has committed his 'treatment' to the ministrations of maleficent doctors.

compass Circle.

waste A term meaning the damage done by a tenant who allows property to deteriorate.

thy grandsire Edward III.

son's son ... sons A reference to Richard's treatment of Edward's sons – in particular Gloucester and John of Gaunt himself.

From forth Out of. Edward III would have arranged for the deposition of Richard, had he perceived the havoc that he was to wreak, once he gained possession of the Crown.

depose thyself Once again Gaunt foresees the future.

thy world Your possessions – the kingdom.

Landlord Another reference to Richard's leasing out of his lands.

bondslave Richard is no longer an absolute monarch, but a mere landlord – subject to the common law, like any other man.

argue's privilege i.e. the privilege that sick men have to speak freely.

admonition Warning.

native residence Richard was renowned for his rosy complexion.

roundly Glibly.

pelican The pelican was supposed to feed its young with its own blood.

tapp'd out A reference to Richard's killing of Gloucester. Thus Richard has 'tapp'd out' the blood of his own kinsman – in a sort of drunken excess. Gloucester's body is seen metaphorically as a wine-cask – containing the blood-royal.

president precedent.

unkindness ... Gaunt wishes that Richard's unkindness (unnatural behaviour) should be as destructive as age itself, and destroy the withered flower, i.e. Richard himself.

sullens The sulks.

impute Attribute.

Harry Duke of Herford i.e. Bolingbroke.

must be Is still to be.

rug-headed Shaggy-headed, with heads like rugs.

kerns Lightly-armed foot-soldiers.

where . . . else St Patrick was supposed to have eliminated snakes and other venomous creatures from Ireland.

tender Loyal.

marriage Bolingbroke was prevented, thanks to the intervention of Richard, from marrying the French king's cousin.

wrinkle Frown.

Accomplish'd . . . hours When he was your age.

gripe Clutch.

letters patent Official documents which acknowledged Bolingbroke's right to inherit from his father all that belonged to the Dukedom of Lancaster.

attorneys-general Legal officers with the power to act in this case.

sue . . . livery To institute legal proceedings to claim possession of lands.

prick Urge.

trow Trust.

great i.e. bursting with a sense of outrage.

Tends that Does what you are about to say concern . . .?

mo More.

prosecute Follow up.

pill'd Pillaged.

blanks The aforementioned 'blank charters'.

benevolences A euphemism for forced loans.

wot not Know not.

this The money so raised.

basely yielded Richard yielded up Brest to the Duke of Brittany. From this cession arose the quarrel with Gloucester.

dissolution Destruction.

sit sore Refers to a steady wind which fills out the sails.

strike A pun: strike our sails; strike a blow.

securely With a false sense of security.

unavoided Unavoidable.

We three . . . thoughts An expression of close friendship. Words are as safe as thoughts.

Brittaine Brittany.

His brother i.e. of the Earl of Arundel.

furnished Provided with arms.

Imp out A term derived from falconry: fresh feathers were 'imped' into a bird's wing to improve its power of flight.

broking pawn The pawnbroker.

in post In all speed.

Ravenspurgh On the N.E. coast – between Hull and Bridlington.

faint Lack courage.

Hold out Provided that my horse holds out.

Act II Scene 2

Richard has departed for Ireland. The Queen is full of presentiments of misfortune and Bushy, one of the King's favourites, attempts to cheer her, but in vain. Greene enters with the news that Bolingbroke, at the head of a force, has landed at Ravenspurgh. We soon learn that he has been joined by Northumberland, Harry Percy, Worcester and other powerful members of the nobility. Rebellion is afoot. York, whom Richard left in charge of the kingdom, is at sixes and sevens – his anxieties are increased by his inability to inform the King of the threatening turn of events. The Duchess of Gloucester has died. Beleaguered, with the King's forces outnumbered, the King's favourites decide to seek refuge: Greene and Bushy go to join the Earl of Wiltshire at Bristol; Bagot will go to Ireland to join the King.

Commentary

The Queen's sadness introduces a new mood into the play: a brooding melancholy and introspection haunt the lines. The Queen's inability to define what troubles her suggests that she is caught up in doom which she is unable to understand. This is a theme which Richard himself will take up later on. Despite our knowledge of his crimes and weakness, we find ourselves gaining – through the Queen's eyes – a different perspective on Richard: she sees him as 'sweet Richard', and her highly-conceited language has a prettiness which barely masks a sense of despair.

Clearly the King's fortunes are declining rapidly, and although Bolingbroke has only just landed, his star is in the ascendant. The static, sad beauty of the early part of the scene is rudely interrupted by the bad news which Greene brings and the state of panic which it induces.

With nothing 'Nothing', as yet, because the sorrow is unborn.
perspectives Probably refers to a toy popular at the time: a picture viewed through glass which produced optical illusions.
Distinguish form Show distinct shapes.
though on thinking . . . think Although to my thinking I have no precise notion of danger in my mind.
heavy nothing The Queen cannot find a cause for her sense of oppression.
conceit Imagination.
'Tis nothing less It is anything but imagination.

reversion The right of possession to a thing when the possessor dies.
repeals himself Withdraws from himself the sentence of exile.
uplifted i.e. in rebellion.
broken his staff Refers to Worcester's staff of office as Steward. Broken as a sign that he had resigned his office.
prodigy Monstrosity. The Queen's fears now have taken on a monstrous reality.
cozening Cheating.
signs of war He is apparently wearing some form of neck-armour.
careful Full of cares.
comfortable Comforting.
crosses Vexations.
sick hour . . . surfeit Present troubles are the result of the King's previous excesses.
your son York's son – Aumerle – had gone to Ireland to join Richard.
cold Indifferent, to the point of becoming hostile.
So my untruth Provided that my disloyalty.
my brother's Gloucester.
sister – cousin A naturalistic touch: York is preoccupied with the death of the Duchess of Gloucester.
my kindred . . . right The demands of kinship urges me to put right.
sits fair Is in the right quarter, to enable messengers to cross from Ireland.
Is near . . . the king i.e. the love we bear the King means that we arouse a corresponding degree of enmity in those that hate him.
lie Rests. If the commons judge the King, so they may expect similar judgement.
little office Scant service.
presages Forebodings.

Act II Scene 3

At the head of his forces, Bolingbroke is on the march across the Cotswolds. He is attended by Northumberland and his son Harry Percy. They are soon joined by Ross and Willoughby. Bolingbroke claims that in marching on the King's force at Berkeley Castle, he seeks the restoration of the Dukedom of Lancaster. Berkeley, and later York, confront Bolingbroke and demand to know the reason for this act of rebellion against Richard.

Bolingbroke reiterates that he comes to claim only what is due to him – by right of succession, on the death of his father. York replies that he has no right to take the law into his own hands, but admits that he is in no position to oppose the superior forces which are ranged against him. He adopts, therefore, a position of reluctant neutrality and offers Bolingbroke 'repose for the night' in Berkeley Castle. The offer is accepted. Bolingbroke then announces his intention to proceed, in due course, to Bristol, in order to 'pluck away' Bushy, Bagot and their accomplices – 'caterpillars of the commonwealth'.

Commentary

We meet Bolingbroke on the march: immediately he is associated with movement and action. As yet, literally and metaphorically, he is in the wilderness. He appears to be a man of few words: even when he does speak at length, he is not given to elaborate conceits – he is clipped and precise. The somewhat sycophantic remarks of Northumberland elicit little response.

York is in an impossible situation but his rebuke to Bolingbroke is brave and timely. Noticeably, Bolingbroke answers the accusation that he has no right to bear arms on his own account and we can sympathize with his desire to regain what is rightfully his: the Dukedom of Lancaster. But he is silent when it comes to accounting for the defiance implicit in breaking the King's banishing order. The fact is that Bolingbroke's claim to have limited aims rings hollow: kingship is in his mind. His whole manner is commanding; he promises to reward the love of his friends from his 'treasury' (a possible Freudian slip); he is apparently considerate towards his uncle, but the commanding tone in his closing remarks is unmistakable: he seems to ask York to accompany him to Bristol, but York really has no option but to obey. Finally, his intention to cleanse the kingdom of Bushy, Bagot, and others of their ilk, is a direct challenge to Richard.

There can be no doubt about Bolingbroke's strength and the King's weakness. It is not just a question of military superiority. As York had predicted, Richard's wresting of the Dukedom of Lancaster from the legal, rightful inheritor, undermined his moral position when Bolingbroke challenges his right to be King. The popularity of Bolingbroke is also a powerful factor in his favour, and one notices that his successes here (and later) come without much expenditure of effort. The kingdom seems to be falling into his lap.

Cotshall Cotswold.
tediousness and process Tedious, slow progress.
hope to joy ... hope enjoy'd To anticipate a joy is only a little less enjoyable than actually having the enjoyment of what is hoped for.

By this i.e. with this thought.

Harry Percy Nicknamed 'Hotspur'.

whencesoever From somewhere or other.

Duke of Herford Hotspur does not recognize Bolingbroke.

approved Tested.

As in a soul As in the possession of a soul that remembers.

stir i.e. what is York doing about the situation.

unfelt Intangible.

which . . . recompense Bolingbroke says that his enriched treasury will provide due reward for their love. Is he anticipating kingship?

infant Immature, but with good hope of prospering.

Lancaster Bolingbroke has inherited his father's title and now demands that it be used.

race Erase.

what lord you will By whatever title you intend to call yourself. Does Berkeley intend an insult, or is he just being cautious?

self-borne Of your own raising, for your own purposes and not on behalf of your country.

deceivable Deceitful.

more "why?" There are yet more questions.

bosom . . . pale-fac'd The country is personified as a frightened woman.

ostentation Ostentatious show of arms.

French Probably refers to the Battle of Crecy.

palsy Paralysis.

what condition What is the nature of my fault.

I come for Lancaster Implies that reclamation of his title is the limit of his ambition.

arms Coat-of-arms.

unthrifts Spendthrifts. Possibly refers to the King himself, or, more likely, to his favourites.

cousin king be King Bolingbroke claims his title by right of succession – as the King claims his kingship.

rouse A hunting term – to start an animal from cover. The image is continued in 'chase' and 'bay' – all terms from stag-hunting.

sue my livery Pursue my claim against the King for possession of the lands of my father.

letters patents Legal documents from the King which give him the right to his title.

distrain'd Seized.

challenge Appeal to.

free Unblemished.

stands . . . upon You are obliged to put matters right.

endowments Possessions.

kind Manner.

Be his own carver i.e. take matters into his own hands in this way.

ill left Left ill-provided.

attach Arrest.

caterpillars Here synonymous with 'parasites'.

Act II Scene 4

The Welsh forces, not hearing any news from the King, are to be dispersed. The Captain speaks of various ill-omens and of his belief that the King is dead. Salisbury comments briefly on the decline in the King's fortunes.

Commentary

This scene reinforces the feeling that Richard is doomed. The disbanding of his Welsh supporters is a disaster for him. The remarks of the Welsh Captain put the King's imminent fall on a cosmic footing – the very heavens portend the fall of kings. This belief derives from the idea that God's universe is disrupted by the deposition of His anointed monarch: disaster and disruption on an earthly scale are mirrored by a corresponding disruption in the heavens. The withered bay-trees (laurel) symbolize the withering of his hopes of victory. Richard's decline and fall is given an aura of inevitability.

hardly With difficulty.
bay-trees ... meteors ... stars All portents of disaster.
lean-look'd Lean-looking.
heavy Sad.
firmament Heavens.
crossly Contrarily.

Revision questions on Act II

1 According to Gaunt and York, what are Richard's failings as a king?
2 What is the dramatic importance of Gaunt's speech which begins: 'Methinks I am a prophet new inspired'?
3 Comment on Richard's attitude towards the dying Gaunt.
4 What is the effect of York's remarks to Richard in Act II, Scene 1?
5 What contribution is made by the Queen to our feelings about Richard?
6 What signs do you find in Act II, Scene 3 that Richard is doomed?
7 Shakespeare 'invented' Act II, Scene 4 – what does it contribute to the play?
8 Compare and contrast the characters of Bolingbroke and Richard on the evidence of the play so far.

9 Do you consider Bolingbroke's return to England to be justified?

10 What weight do you give to the King's Divine Right to rule in the light of his manifest unsuitability for kingship?

Act III Scene 1

Bolingbroke, now arrived at Bristol Castle, outlines the crimes of Bushy, Greene and other prisoners, before sending them to execution. They are accused of having corrupted the King; of destroying the royal marriage; and of contributing to the exile and disinheriting of Bolingbroke himself. The discredited favourites leave, cursing Bolingbroke. The Queen is to be treated well. Bolingbroke departs to fight with Glendower.

Commentary

Bolingbroke gives an impression of decisiveness as he delivers sentence of death on the King's favourites. We may be surprised to find that Bristol Castle is in his hands and that he is already in a position to mete out punishment to the offenders. Events are running his way with gathering impetus and surprising speed.

Arguably here, he is already behaving as if he were king. A cynic might find his protestations of ridding the state of 'caterpillars' and his pretensions of protecting the interests of the King to be a shade hypocritical.

urging Too much insistence upon.
charity Kindness.
happy Fortunate.
blood i.e. his birth.
lineaments Beautiful appearance.
clean Utterly.
Broke . . . bed i.e. destroyed the King's marital harmony.
sigh'd . . clouds Bolingbroke's sighs increased the volume of foreign clouds. A rather fanciful exaggeration!
signories Manors, estates.
Dispark'd Threw open my parklands.
windows . . . coat The family coat of arms was torn from the windows, where they were emblazoned.
imprese Family motto, normally attached to a crest.
injustice Those who perpetrate this injustice.
intreated Treated.
commends Greeting.

at large In full.
Glendor Owen Glendower – a Welsh favourite.

Act III Scene 2

Richard returns to England and disembarks on the coast of North Wales. He has heard of the progress of Bolingbroke through his land and greets England in a state of high emotion. Richard is optimistically relying on God's support to help him overcome his foes. Carlisle and Aumerle urge that God's will must be performed by human agents, and that all tangible means of support should be eagerly embraced. Richard's confidence in Divine protection is maintained until he hears of the collapse of his Welsh forces. At this news he pales, but he regains his composure when he remembers that York still holds command of a considerable force, upon which he believes he can still rely. The arrival of Scroop ushers in more bad news: Bolingbroke enjoys universal popularity and some of his favourites have been executed. At once, a mood of blank despair seizes Richard. He can foresee only his defeat and death. There is some flicker of hope when Aumerle reminds him of York and his army. But this vanishes when Scroop reports that York has capitulated and gone over to Bolingbroke. Despair returns; Richard dismisses his forces, and, devoid of hope, sets out for Flint Castle.

Commentary

It would not be too strong to say that by the end of this scene we are forced to reassess our opinion of Richard. The Queen's description of her husband in Act II, Scene 2 presented him in a more sympathetic light than perhaps his actions seem to deserve – we had seen little evidence of her 'sweet Richard' – but as his fortunes decline, so we find that he assumes a pathetic dignity. By the end of the play it is possible to see him not simply as a 'bad king', but more as a tragic figure.

Richard begins by greeting England and expressing a belief that he cannot be deposed because he is possessed of Divine protection. It is this faith in his inviolability which prompts Richard to believe that he may rely upon the Almighty to send His 'angels' to defend the royal person. Carlisle's words, to the effect that God helps those who help themselves, do not impress Richard, who identifies his return from Ireland with the coming of daylight.

As one piece of bad news follows upon another, so with momentary fluctuations into optimism, the King's mood gravitates towards despair. He ends by discharging his followers, ironically in respect of his earlier statements, seeing himself invested with night in contrast to 'Bolingbroke's fair day'.

If we attempt to analyse why our response to Richard undergoes a change, we may first note that, quite simply, he speaks some of the finest verse which Shakespeare ever wrote. Furthermore, his speeches give evidence of an insight into his situation which Richard has never previously demonstrated. It is as if the awareness that kingship has departed from him has forced him to consider himself afresh: devoid of the certainty of Divine protection and stripped of the material trappings of power, Richard finds that he is but a man. In these circumstances, and with this insight, the 'self and vain conceit' of monarchy becomes a bitter joke – and Death is the jester who has the last laugh. The Crown is 'hollow' in more senses than one.

In this scene, towards the end, there hangs about Richard a sense of passive suffering which embodies a deal of self-pity. But it is self-pity which is enshrined in verse of such invention and exquisite sensibility that it moves us to tears rather than embarrassment. The metaphor of Death, his court, his little pin boring through the castle wall – until 'farewell king', has a horrid clarity and truth which personalizes and universalizes Richard's predicament. In such moments, Richard speaks not only for himself but also for all men and their pretensions.

brooks Enjoys.
do thee favours Caress you.
sense Appetite.
heavy-gaited Heavy-footed.
toads Believed to be poisonous creatures.
annoyance Harm.
conjuration Solemn invocation.
Power i.e. Divine Power.
yields Offers.
heaven would . . . not What the heavens wish to occur, we are not willing to bring about.
remiss Neglectful.
security Carelessness.
Discomfortable Discouraging.
Behind the globe i.e. at night, when the sun is illuminating the other side of the world. Note the suggestion that the sun's absence may be likened to the King's absence, whilst he is in Ireland.
fires Illuminates.

with the Antipodes i.e. amongst foreign nations – in Richard's case in Ireland.

blushing i.e. with shame.

balm Sacred oil.

breath ... men i.e. the talk of all the men in the world.

press'd Forced to join his army.

Did triumph ... face A moment ago, I was flushed with confidence in the thought that twenty thousand men were ready to fight for me.

that will Who wish to be.

kingdom ... care If you come to tell me that my kingdom is lost, what need I worry, for you come to tell me that I lose that which is the source of care.

fellow Equal.

Cry Speak all you know of.

clap their female joints Thrust their feminine (because of their youth) limbs.

beadsmen Pensioners, who offered prayers (on a rosary) in return for alms.

yew Doubly deadly because yews were used to make bows, and yew-leaves are poisonous.

manage Wield.

bills Weapons which were part-pike, part-battle-axe.

Measure our confines March across our territories.

peaceful Unopposed.

Judases Judas Iscariot, whose name was a by-word for treachery.

spotted Tainted with wickedness.

his property Its nature.

peace ... hands i.e. they have not shaken hands with Bolingbroke; they have made their peace with their Maker – by being executed.

model Mound or shape, such as may be found on top of a grave – roughly in the shape of a human body.

rounds Surrounds, encircles.

antic Jester, buffoon. It was a commonplace to picture Death as a jester, who grinned mockingly at mankind and his aspirations.

state Stateliness.

To monarchize To play the king.

Infusing him Puffing him up.

humour'd thus Thus amused. May refer to a king, or to Death – or both, i.e. whilst the king is enjoying this frame of mind, Death to entertain himself, comes ...

Cover your heads Do not stand bareheaded as a mark of respect to someone who is only a man – such an action is, in fact, a mere mockery.

Gives ... foe In your weakness the enemy can find strength.

Fear ... fight If you are fearful, you will be killed – fighting cannot lead to any worse fate.

And fight ... breath To die fighting is to conquer death, whereas to fear death is to acknowledge, in the manner of a slave, the superiority of death.

learn . . . limb i.e. use that part of what you have left as if it were the
   whole. Make the best of your resources. Dramatic irony: Aumerle does
   not know of his father's capitulation.
change Exchange.
complexion Appearance.
inclination i.e. what the weather will be.
Upon his party On his side.
Beshrew A mild oath.
sweet . . . to despair Richard 'rebukes' Aumerle for distracting him
   from the habit of despair, which he was so easily beginning to acquire.
ear Plough.
some hope Richard implies that he is a lost cause.
double wrong Flattery is doubly wrong because it is an evil in itself, and
   wrong when it brings woe and not consolation.

Act III Scene 3

Bolingbroke arrives at Flint Castle, where he learns of the disintegration of the Welsh forces, and that the King has landed from
Ireland. He is, however, surprised to hear that Richard has
taken refuge within the castle walls. A parley is sounded and
Bolingbroke makes public declaration of his loyalty; he requires
only that the banishment be revoked and that his lands be
returned.

Richard appears on the castle walls and demands to know the
reasons for Bolingbroke's insubordination and treachery. Northumberland states Bolingbroke's demands and repeats his profes-
sions of loyalty. If the King will grant these 'requests', Bolingbroke
will disband his army.

Recognizing the impossibility of his situation, Richard
acknowledges, to Aumerle, that his kingship is over. In a mood
of anger and grief he begs ironically to be granted permission to
live out his life as a hermit: exchanging courtly opulence for
humble simplicity. He admits that he talks 'idly', and, in the
confrontation which follows, Richard brushes aside Bolingbroke's courtesies and agrees to go to London – 'we must do
what force will have us do.'

Commentary

There is no reason to doubt the limited aims of Bolingbroke's
rebelliousness – his demands are 'reasonable', even just.
Richard's interpretation of the rebellion is equally tenable, and
his speech, asserting the heinous nature of such actions and
embodying a prophecy of the consequences, is regally delivered.

Bolingbroke is no Machiavelli – the king could compromise; the rights could be restored. Bolingbroke could pay homage.

But all this is to ignore the realities of the situation – and this the King cannot do. Aumerle's invitation to duplicity seems to affront Richard – implicit in the suggestion is the truth that the King is so impotent that he *needs* to indulge in chicanery. A king without absolute obedience (derived from Divine authority) is, in fact, no king at all. To our ears, the refusal, in the end, to compromise seems unreasonable; to Richard, however, comes the sudden realization that it is all or nothing. As his first speech has indicated, the mere act of rebellion is wrong – and the fact that from a position of strength, it is Bolingbroke who is dictating the terms, leads to a complete collapse of confidence. Bolingbroke, whether he likes it or not (and one suspects he does like it), is given the crown. In a speech of haunting beauty, and bracketed by some bitter irony, Richard sees himself, in fantasy, exchanging the trappings of royalty (which have always meant much to him) for the garb of a simple, holy man. He weeps tears of self-pity and provokes tears from his friends. Confronted with possibilities of statesmanship and/or duplicity, he rejects both for highly conceited indulgence of poetry. It is characteristic and it is moving, but, in his predicament, it lacks effectiveness.

Such are the realities: Richard has the poetry but not the power: Bolingbroke has few words, but, possibly almost to his own embarrassment, he has the power. For the moment, God would appear to be on the side of the big battalions.

The time . . . head's length York suggests that such disrespect as the omission of the King's title would have led to Northumberland's being 'shortened' by the length of his head!

taking so the head Taking such liberties, as well as its literal meaning.

the heavens A reminder that rebellion risks Divine wrath.

Royally! Bolingbroke expresses surprise that Richard is in Flint Castle. Here Shakespeare diverges from his source (Holinshed).

limits i.e. within the castle walls.

rude Coarse, flinty.

ribs Walls.

his i.e. the castle's.

ruin'd ears Refers to the loopholes and battered casements.

lay Settle.

stooping duty Bowing the knee in homage.

tottered Tattered, ragged.

Our fair . . . perus'd So that it may be seen how well equipped we are.

thund'ring shock It was believed that a thunderstorm was the result of the collision of fire and water.

Parle A trumpet is sounded to signify a conference.

portal Gateway.

the eagle A symbol of royalty. The eagle was supreme amongst birds.

Controlling i.e. which controls the wills of others.

Unless Without.

torn i.e. torn up their bonds of allegiance, which are imagined to have been written on parchment.

vassal Subservient.

The purple testament War is imagined to be like a will, which once opened comes into force. Purple – 'bloodstained'.

crown . . . crowns A pun: crown in the sense of a king's crown, and meaning 'heads.'

the flower . . . face i.e. the flower-bedecked fields of England.

civil . . . uncivil i.e. civil war which is anything but polite.

honourable tomb Refers to the tomb of Edward III in Westminster Abbey.

lineal royalties That which is due to be by inheritance.

party On your own behalf, as an interested person in the agreement.

barbed Armour-clad.

commends Hand over.

scope Permission.

almsman One who lives on charity. Refers here particularly to a 'holy man', or hermit.

figur'd Ornamented.

palmer A pilgrim who had made a pilgrimage to the Holy Land.

lodge Beat down.

wantons i.e. make light of our woes.

pretty match i.e. have a tear-shedding contest.

fretted Worn out for us.

King Bolingbroke Richard acknowledges in this irony the reality of his situation.

make a leg Bow the knee.

base court The lower castle yard.

Phaeton The son of the sun-god, Apollo. Phaeton tricked his father into allowing him to drive the chariot of the sun, properly Apollo's prerogative. Phaeton proved incompetent and came too near the surface of the earth, which was only saved from incineration by the intervention of Zeus, who destroyed him with a thunderbolt. Phaeton is thus a symbol of those who seek to rise above their proper station.

jades Broken-down cart-horses.

want their remedies Lack the power to give any assistance.

too young Historically, Richard and Bolingbroke were both thirty-three years old.

Act III Scene 4

In the Duke of York's garden, the Queen still grieves. A gardener and two servants enter, and are soon discussing the political events of the day. Bolingbroke has removed from the 'garden of England' the choking weeds (the King's favourites) which threatened the good order of the commonwealth. But Bolingbroke himself has exceeded his authority and deposed the King, who, of course, should be the 'gardener-in-chief' of the realm. In not keeping in check those trees which have too much sap, the King has permitted them to become 'too great and growing': an exact metaphor for the rise of Bolingbroke. The Queen, who has overheard all this, intervenes: she cannot believe that her Richard has been defeated. But the gardener tells her that her husband's downfall is common knowledge. In sorrow and anger the Queen makes for London to meet with her husband.

Commentary

This scene furthers the plot by showing us the Queen receiving the news of Richard's defeat. Its importance, however, is to give us a glimpse of ordinary men going about their daily business. Certain conclusions may be drawn. First, whatever ambiguities and treacheries may occupy the high and mighty, common Englishmen are fundamentally a healthy breed. The 'garden of the state' may be ill-managed; but they do their duty despite the difficulties. Secondly, the masses support the actions of Bolingbroke, who roots out the 'weeds' in the state. Thirdly, they appreciate that Bolingbroke usurps the true function of the King – and they regard news of his actions as 'black tidings'. Fundamentally loyal, and appreciating the necessity for firm government, they would rather that weeding operations went under the overall direction of Richard. Finally, their sympathy for the distraught Queen (despite her farewell curse) shows a common humanity which elevates them to a high moral plane.

rubs Hindrances on a bowling green which impede the roll of the bowl.
bias Bowls are loaded with lead, which causes them to veer to one side
 – this is called the 'bias'.
measure Rhythm.
My wretchedness . . . pins I'll bet my wretchedness against a row of
 pins.
Against At the time of.
too lofty Some of the sprays are growing too well, at the expense of the
 general good.

commonwealth State. Here, and elsewhere, Shakespeare likens the state to a garden.

noisome Poisonous, harmful.

pale Enclosure. Gardens were fenced in by palings.

knots A name given to elaborately laid-out gardens – popular with the Elizabethans.

caterpillars Echoes Bolingbroke's remark in Act II, Scene 3: Bushy, Bagot, Greene are 'The caterpillars of the commonwealth,/ Which I have sworn to weed and pluck away.'

seem'd in . . . him up i.e. whilst they seemed to be supporting the King, in fact they were eating him up. In other words, they were parasites.

over-proud Too luxuriant.

confound Destroy.

bearing Fruitful.

press'd Tortured to death. Pressing a victim with a heavy weight was a method of extracting confessions.

old Adam By tradition Adam was a gardener.

rude Unlearned.

second fall Adam was cursed by God when he was ejected from Eden. The gardener has just referred to the fall of Richard.

vanities Vain people.

embassage Ambassadorial message.

I would . . . curse If cursing my skill might in any way help you, then I wish it might aid you in your predicament ('state').

rue A herb associated, in 'the language of flowers', with repentance.

ruth Pity.

Revision questions on Act III

1 From his treatment of the King's favourites, what impression do you gain of Bolingbroke?

2 In detail, outline the bad news that Richard receives when he lands on the coast of Wales.

3 Demonstrate, using quotations, Richard's fluctuations of mood in Act III, Scene 2.

4 Discuss the influence of Carlisle, Aumerle and Scroope in Act III, Scene 2. Differentiate between them, if possible, in terms of their impact on Richard.

5 Why do you think that Richard surrenders so easily to Bolingbroke?

6 How sincere do you find Bolingbroke's protestations of loyalty, in the light of his actions?

7 Argue, in your own words, Bolingbroke's case for rebelling against the King.

8 What contribution to the play is made by Act III, Scene 4?

9 On the evidence of the play so far, do you think that Boling-broke has the necessary qualities to make a good king? What are his strengths and/or weaknesses?
10 How far do you find, in Act III, that Richard has engaged your sympathies? Give reasons for your answer.

Act IV Scene 1

In Westminster Hall, before the asembled Parliament, the mat-ter of Gloucester's death is revived. Bolingbroke summons Bagot, who accuses Aumerle of the deed. Aumerle vehemently denies it, throwing down his gage. Bolingbroke refuses permis-sion for Bagot to accept the challenge, but there follows an undignified series of accusations and denials. Eventually, Bolingbroke suspends all challenges pending the return of Nor-folk from banishment. At this point, Carlisle tells the assembled company that Norfolk has died in exile.

York enters to inform Bolingbroke that Richard is prepared to abdicate. Carlisle denounces the whole proceedings: no sub-ject has the right to judge the King, and he prophesies that England will undergo a period of terrible bloodshed and civil disorder should the usurpation be countenanced. Northum-berland promptly calls for the arrest of Carlisle.

Richard is summoned before Bolingbroke. The King is unable to come to terms with his own deposition: he is in a confused state of mind, and harping again on his own demise, he formally hands over the crown to Bolingbroke. He is, however, unable to read out a document which is presented to him by Northum-berland, confessing his grievous crimes and Bolingbroke decides to let the matter rest. Richard is then conveyed to the Tower.

As Bolingbroke departs, announcing preparations for his coro-nation, the Abbot of Westminster, Carlisle and Aumerle talk of 'laying a plot' against Bolingbroke.

Commentary

When Bolingbroke demands that Bagot tells what he knows of Gloucester's death, there follows a series of challenges which threaten to get out of hand. As a foretaste in miniature of Bolingbroke's regime, the chaotic hurling down of gages does not bode well for the future of England. The episode is, of course, reminiscent of the opening scene of the play. In com-parison, Richard's handling of a similar situation seems more dignified. Though his position was weak, he found the authority and the words to restore order; furthermore, the staging of the tournament was a fitting and dignified way of resolving the issue between Bolingbroke and Norfolk. On this occasion, Bolingbroke does not really establish himself until helped by the sobering news of Norfolk's death – at one point disintegration is imminent, as Aumerle, Fitzwater, Surrey and Percy berate one another without restraint. But Bolingbroke's authority prevails nonetheless.

York's announcement that Richard is prepared to abdicate provokes Carlisle into asserting that subjects do not have the right to judge Richard. To overthrow Richard is an act of sacrilege. From this 'heinous, black, obscene deed', Carlisle foresees, will flow a disordered England, riddled with internecine strife. At this point in the play, Shakespeare ensures that we should not lose sight of the enormity of what is being enacted before us. Northumberland's response is to arrest Carlisle – the reality of force is demonstrated. But for all the 'management' of power-politics displayed in this scene, Carlisle's vehemently stated convictions remain fixed in the mind. They have the unmistakable ring of truth.

Richard hands over the crown: once again the dictates of power prevail. Richard himself enters a state of limbo. Nonetheless, he 'gives the heavy weight from off my head' in a speech which has the formality of a coronation. He is, however, unable to submit to the humiliation of reading out a list of his 'crimes'. To his credit, Bolingbroke shows some mercy to Richard and, despite the urgings of the brutal Northumberland, the matter is dropped.

In this bleak situation, we find out sympathies drawn even more powerfully towards Richard. Bolingbroke is laconic, to say the least, and Northumberland is simply a bully. Thus our attention is forced on to Richard and his suffering. When a looking-glass is fetched, and the King contemplates his own face, we experience a mixture of emotions. There is something narcissistic about his commenting on his own beauty, which reminds us of the vain 'giddy' Richard of old. But the moment also possesses extreme poignancy as Richard stares at himself: he recognizes the outward appearance, but cannot believe that the appearance no longer betokens the reality of his kingship. He dashes the looking-glass to the ground: this gesture symbolically unites appearance and reality – a shattered face is now at one with a shattered kingship, and the beautiful appearance no longer lives to mock the ugly reality of his situation.

The scene ends ominously: Henry Bolingbroke may be planning his coronation, but others are planning his demise. Already Carlisle's prophecies are coming true – trouble is on the horizon.

Clearly Bolingbroke has not had things his own way in this scene: what was 'meant' to happen, namely a smooth transference of power has not, in fact, taken place. True, what Bolingbroke intended to happen has happened – but the feelings are all wrong. From his point of view, the death of Gloucester 'debate' became an unseemly, acrimonious squabble; Richard has not publicly 'confessed'; Richard has refused to go quietly and has engaged our sympathies – he has been embarrassing; a counter-plot is afoot. All this is in contrast to Bolingbroke's rise to power, which was notably without hitches.

wrought it Inspired the King to have it performed.

timeless Untimely.

of length . . . reacheth Of sufficient length to reach.

base man i.e. this 'nobody'.

fair stars Refers to the belief that a man's destiny was governed by the planets, which predominated in the heavens at the time of his birth.

On equal terms Aumerle refuses to lower himself to answer such charges, by accepting the challenge of the low-born Bagot.

attainder Accusation.

Excepting one A calculated insult to Bolingbroke.

sympathy i.e. equivalence of rank.

appeal Challenge.

I task . . . like I command the earth to bear my gage in a similar challenge.

in presence Present

boy A contemptuous reference.

this new world i.e. the new world which has come into being by virtue of Bolingbroke's rebellion.

repeal'd Recalled.

signories Estates.

Jesu Christ Refers to Norfolk's Crusading zeal.

bosom . . . Abraham A euphemism for death.

plume-plucked Humiliated. According to Aesop, a crow bedecked himself with stolen feathers. Other birds shamed him by plucking them away.

heir . . . his throne After pronouncing Henry Bolingbroke his heir, Richard promptly abdicates.

Learn Teach.

forfend . . . God May God forbid it.

Herford . . . Herford The suggestion is that Bolingbroke is being a traitor to himself in being treacherous to his King.

tumultuous wars Refers prophetically to the Wars of the Roses.

kin . . . kin . . . kind . . . kind i.e. families will be rent asunder in conflict, and Englishmen will fight Englishmen.

The field of Golgotha 'The place of a skull', see Matthew, 27,33.

house . . . house The Royal House of York and Lancaster.

Of On the charge of.

suit Proposal.

sureties 'Guarantees' that they will appear before the court to stand trial.

at your helping hands Bolingbroke expects little love or help at their hands.

favours A pun: favours are 'faces', and it refers to those to whom Richard gave literal 'favours', in earlier days.

clerk The clerk gives the responses to the priest's prayers.

tired majesty Your weariness with the office of King.

owes Has.

filling one another Presumably by alternately rising and falling. Rising and falling buckets in a well are a symbol of the rising and falling of a man's fortune.

'tend Accompany.

ay, no; no, ay A pun which depends on the similarity of sound between *Ay* meaning yes, and *I*, the first person.

duty's rites Homage, when, ceremonially, a subject declares his loyalty to the monarch.

deem Judge.

troop Gathering.

read a lecture Publicly confess.

cracking . . . an oath Breaking the solemn oath of allegiance.

bait Worry, cause myself anxiety.

Pilate The Roman governor who tried and condemned Christ.

sort Company of.

insulting Triumphing, without modesty.

I have no name Richard was actually baptised John.

fac'd Put a good face on so much foolishness.

out-fac'd Stared down.

shivers Splinters.

The shadow . . . your face Bolingbroke says that the darkness of grief has destroyed the beauteous image of Richard's face.

boon Favour.

Conveyers Euphemism for 'thieves'.

pageant Spectacle.

blot i.e. Bolingbroke.

take the sacrament To make the vow particularly binding.

Act V Scene 1

In a London street, the Queen awaits her husband, who is on his way to the Tower. Richard arrives, and she comments on his woebegone appearance and expresses surprise that he is taking his 'correction' so mildly. Sadly, Richard says that she should think of him as if he were dead. Northumberland arrives to say that Bolingbroke has changed his mind: Richard must now go to Pomfret Castle, not the Tower. Richard prophesies that Northumberland will not be content to be subordinate to Bolingbroke.

Richard and the Queen take their leave. Bolingbroke has effected a 'divorce' between them: Richard must go to the North; the Queen must go to France.

Commentary

Richard and the Queen meet for the last time. There is a sad exchange of farewells: circumstances have forced a divorce between Richard and his wife. Shakespeare uses the Queen's love and grief to engage our sympathies for the King. Initially, the Queen notices the changes which have occurred in Richard's appearance. In reply, Richard pretends not to recognize his wife, addressing her as 'fair woman', and he goes on to suggest that she should go to France and enter a religious order. This provokes the Queen to respond angrily that Richard has been weakened in mind, as well as physically, and she cannot understand why he accepts his 'correction' so mildly. In all probability she is attempting to bludgeon him out of the mood of despondency, which seems to enshroud him, but Richard has lost the will to stand up for himself. He only looks for death to take him, and he moves towards it as if he were the chief character in story. At one point he actually asks his wife to tell his 'lamentable tale' after he has gone, and 'send the hearers weeping to their beds'. It is typical of Richard to dramatize his own predicament and symptomatic of deep despair.

These melancholy reflections are brutally interrupted by Northumberland, whose callous insensitivity serves to heighten the pathos still further. But the effect on Richard is to stimulate a fierce prophecy on the fate of Northumberland. This emphasizes yet again the heinousness of usurpation, and it looks forward to a time when Bolingbroke and Northumberland come into conflict. The prophetic utterances in the play are important, for they put present actions into a time-context – thus Richard's deposition and death are not the end of the story, but rather we are witnessing the dawn of an era of bloodshed and civil disorder. A moral point is also raised: how justified is rebellion in the light of what happens later? Richard may have been a bad king and have committed outrageous crimes, but the destruction consequent upon his death should give pause – even to the most outraged. Shakespeare is a powerful advocate of order.

Julius Caesar's . . . tower According to legend the Tower of London was built by Julius Caesar.

ill-erected Built for an evil purpose.

rebellious earth The Queen imagines that the very ground she stands on is imbued with the spirit of rebellion.

model where old Troy The Queen likens her husband to the ruins of Troy after it was sacked by the Greeks.

map Image.

beauteous inn i.e. Richard.

hard-favour'd Ugly.

alehouse i.e. Bolingbroke.

new world's Heavenly.

profane Worldly.

shape Outward appearance.

the lion The king of beasts – hence a symbol of royalty.

the rod i.e. the rod of chastisement.

on rage On the wrath which you suffer.

if . . . beasts If my adversaries had been other than beasts.

prepare thee Make preparations to go to France.

betid Occurred.

to quite their griefs To return, on your own account, the sad tales which you have been told.

senseless brands The burning logs which are devoid of feeling.

moving Literally moving, and moving in the sense of emotionally affecting.

some i.e. some logs.

Pomfret Pontefract, in Yorkshire.

there is order ta'en Arrangements have been made.

gathering head Coming to a head (like a boil).

break Erupt.

Being ne'er . . . urged On the slightest pretext.

converts Turns.

turns Brings either to the king, or to the person who makes the king, or to both.

worthy Merited.

unkiss the oath i.e. with a kiss, revoke the kiss I gave you as part of the marriage-oath.

pines the clime Oppresses the countryside.

Hollowmass All Saints' Day, November 1st.

little policy Politically ill-advised.

be ne'er the near Than to be in proximity with one another and never be able to meet.

Twice for one step Richard will equal the Queen's grief by groaning twice for each step he takes!
woe wanton We make woe wasteful.

Act V Scene 2

The Duke of York and his wife discuss the departure of Richard and the coronation of Bolinbroke. Richard was the recipient of the crowd's insults: Bolingbroke received adulation. But despite his humiliation, Richard was dignified.

Aumerle enters. He has been demoted. York notices a paper which his son is at pains to conceal. He seizes it from Aumerle and reads of the plot to kill the King (Bolingbroke) at Oxford. York, unhesitatingly, and despite the angry protests of his wife, decides that he must go to the King and tell him of the plot. As a last resort, the Duchess urges her son to ride before his father to the King and demand pardon.

Commentary

The seeds of disorder have already been sown and the prophecy of the Bishop of Carlisle is bearing fruit. We find here that a family is divided. It is an extraordinary spectacle: a father is prepared to denounce his son, in the knowledge that he is probably condemning him to death. York is faithfully following his oath of loyalty to the King – at the price of the bonds of kinship. If we accept the scene at face value, then it becomes a powerful symbol of disorder – father against son, and wife against husband. It arises as a consequence of Bolingbroke's assumption of power.

cousins'... London The respective returns to London from Flint of Bolingbroke and Richard.
stop Point.
rude Brutal.
misgoverned Ill-mannered.
seem'd to know Bolingbroke and his horse are of one mind.
that all... said at once It appeared as though people were like painted images, with the words depicted issuing from their mouths. Such images were painted on tapestries in Shakespeare's time.
idly Casually.
bent Turned.
gentle Noble.
combating Richard's face betrayed a conflict between tears of sorrow – and smiles of patient endurance.

barbarism i.e. savages.
bound . . . contents We bind ourself with calm contentment.
fealty Loyalty.
violets A synonym for 'favourites'.
as lief . . . as one I would as soon be nothing as one (of Bolingbroke's favoured ones).
justs Tournaments.
triumph Victory processions.
hold Take place.
seal The sign of the ratification of an agreement – usually made by an impression in wax, to which a ribbon was attached.
without Outside.
band . . . apparel The Duchess thinks that it is probably a bond which Aumerle has taken out, in order to borrow money to buy some clothes for the forthcoming celebrations.
Bound to himself York rightly points out that if the Duchess is correct then the money-lender would be in possession of the bond, not Aumerle.
appeach Inform against.
thine own Your own son.
teeming . . . time I am well past the age of child-bearing.
mine age My old age.
set . . . hands Signed their names, or written in their own handwriting.
none Not be one of them.
groan'd Suffered the pangs of childbirth.
Spur post Ride with all possible haste.

Act V Scene 3

Bolingbroke (King Henry IV) laments the waywardness of his son, who keeps company with a dissolute crew in the low taverns and brothels of London. Aumerle arrives to plead for pardon but he is interrupted by York, who denounces his son as a traitor. Next, the Duchess enters to beg, on her knees, that the King will pardon her son. Henry gives his pardon but condemns to death Aumerle's co-conspirators.

Commentary

In the previous scene we witnessed the disintegration of York's family and here we note that the newly-crowned King also has dissension in his own family. Henry's son is wayward and thoughtless of his father. Shakespeare examines the relationship between King Henry and his son (Hal) in Henry IV Parts 1 and 2.

Aumerle's request for pardon wins the heart of the King,

despite York's denunciation of his son. Henry is also swayed by the powerful pleas of the Duchess – he behaves magnanimously. But his magnanimity does not stretch to include the other conspirators, who are to be dogged to destruction.

Much adverse criticism has been levelled at this scene, and the tone, which rises to a level of near farce at times, is strangely inappropriate bearing in mind the nature of the accusations and the possible consequences. Henry himself seems amused by the exaggerated behaviour of the Duchess, who refuses to rise from her knees. However, it is undeniable that the conflict of loyalties exhibited by York, who is apparently willing to forgo the ties of kinship out of devotion to the King, is basically a serious issue: it would probably be a mistake to play up the comic element at its expense.

beat our watch Attacks our law-officers (watchmen).
passengers Passers-by, pedestrians.
wanton Wastrel.
stews Brothels.
elder years When he grows up.
happily With good luck.
cleave Stick firmly to.
Unless Unless you grant me a pardon.
on the first i.e. 'intended'.
thy after-love Your love for ever afterwards.
safe Harmless.
sheer Pure.
immaculate Faultless.
fountain Spring.
this stream Refers to Aumerle, who has become defiled, and corrupted the purity of his origins.
converts Changes.
thy abundant goodness The imagery here suggests that the abundant 'stream' of goodness, which flows from York (and is revealed by his being prepared to denounce his own son), has washed away the vileness of his 'muddy', treacherous son. 'Digressing' means transgressing.
So . . . bawd If you forgive him, then my virtuousness will be but the protector of his wickedness. York persists in his belief that Aumerle should be executed.
spend Waste.
scraping Thrifty.
Mine honour . . . dies My honour is maintained only if he dies.
my sham'd life . . . lies I must live in shame, if he is permitted to live on in dishonour.
Thou . . . life If you spare him, you kill me.

'**The Beggar and the King**' A reference to a popular ballad of
Shakespeare's day. King Cophetua fell in love with a beggar-maid.

rest rest sound The rest of the body remains healthy.

itself Its own offspring, kith and kin.

dugs Breasts.

would be denied Wishes to be denied what he appears to ask for.

thy tongue to teach i.e. responsible for teaching you to speak.

'**pardonne moy**' May I be excused.

chopping Altering the meaning of words.

Thine eye . . . there Your looks tell me that you are beginning to pity
me; let your words follow your looks.

piteous . . . ear Listen to what your pitying heart tells you.

rehearse Utter.

doth not pardon . . . pardon strong Does not make two separate
pardons, but makes one pardon the mightier.

God make thee new Aumerle did in fact reform, and performed
heroically at Agincourt (1415), under Henry V.

Act V Scene 4

The King has apparently been calling for the death of Richard,
who has become a 'living fear' to him. Exton decides to oblige his
King by murdering Richard.

Commentary

On the inspiration of a chance remark by Bolingbroke, Sir Piers
Exton is prepared to murder Richard. Given the opportunity,
there are always men available 'to do the dirty-work'. Doubtless,
he hopes for advancement. We have seen that Henry's reign is
already full of discord: both on the family level and within the
'family' of the nation: at such times, butchers like Exton come
into their own.

wistly look'd on me Looked intently at me.

As . . . say As if he meant to say.

Act V Scene 5

Richard, alone in Pomfret Castle, is attempting to come to terms
with his captivity – but he fails: his imprisonment constantly
confirms in his mind that he is a mere 'thing': a Jack of the
Clock, who moves according to the dictates of Bolingbroke.
Music plays, but its harmonies only serve to emphasize the
harshness of Richard's situation. A groom enters, who hails

Richard as 'Royal prince', and tells how on his coronation day Bolingbroke rode upon Richard's horse. A jailer brings food but refuses to taste before Richard – it's probably poisoned. Finally, Exton rushes in with murderers. Despite a struggle, Richard is struck down and dies. Exton fearfully contemplates the enormity of what he has done.

Commentary

Alone in Pomfret Castle, Richard cannot muse himself into contentment with being, and possessing, 'nothing'. The struggle to come to terms with himself and his situation is arduous, but we can perhaps admire the man who, even in this extremity, seeks to reconcile himself to a bare prison cell. Music is no help to the stricken Richard, but whilst it plays, two important insights come to him: first, he acknowledges his own folly which contributed to his downfall ('I wasted time, now doth time waste me'). It is important to his dignity as a man and a tragic figure that he dies knowing this. This honest admission of folly enhances our opinion of him. Also, Richard realizes, and is cheered by, the knowledge that he has at least one person who cares for him, and has taken the trouble to play for him. The Groom emphasizes this point and shows Richard a kindness and sympathy which earns his gratitude. As the Queen would have wished, Richard berates himself for bearing the impositions of 'jaunting Bolingbroke'. 'I was not made a horse' is a statement which marks the acquisition of some fighting spirit.

Richard has been preoccupied with thoughts of death, but when it comes he does not go as a lamb to the slaughter. The final movement of the scene is introduced by the arrival of the sinister Keeper: ominously, he refuses to taste the food which he brings; the hapless Richard can read the sign: death is near. He does not surrender and beats the Keeper. The scene ends in violence, with Richard fighting for his life – and we respect him for it. Exton, however, the murder completed, hates himself for what he has done.

hammer it out Strive hard to pursue the idea.
I'll prove . . . the father The idea is that the male will be his reason and the female will be his heart. From a union of heart and mind his hope is to beget a generation of thoughts with which to 'populate' his cell.
still-breeding Self-generating.
humours Temperaments.
set the word . . . the word i.e. one text tends to contradict another.

postern A small gate. The gist of this is that Christ's remark 'Come little ones' (which is all-welcoming) seems to be contradicted by the remark about the camel, which stresses the difficulty of entering the Kingdom.

nails Finger-nails. Aspiring thoughts provoke the need for a miracle – that he will be able to scratch his way through the castle walls. An 'unlikely wonder', indeed!

ragged Rough-hewn.

die i.e. the ambitious thoughts die at their moment of proud conception.

silly Simple, harmless.

Bearing . . . the like Comforting themselves with the thought that they are not the first to have suffered in this manner.

And . . . I am And so I become one (in my imagination).

penury Poverty.

being nothing i.e. by dying.

proportion Harmony.

daintiness Refinement, discrimination.

string Stringed instrument. Music increases the pathos here.

state and time My kingdom and the way I used time.

jar His sighs sound out the passing time: they resemble the ticking of a clock.

watches The minute-marking on a clock-face. It cannot be denied that this conceit is extremely obscure, and it may indicate Richard's state of mind in that he seems to lose his way as he proceeds with it. Richard sees himself as having nothing to occupy his mind except to watch time passing. From this, he proceeds to liken his griefs to minutes, by which his time may be measured. His sighs become like the regular ticks of a clock. But, the face of his clock is his own face (i.e. he sees himself as a clock, at this stage). Thus, to note the passing of time it is only necessary to look at his eyes, which resemble the rim of a clock face – the point where time is actually measured. As he wipes away the tears with his fingers, they come to resemble the sweeping hands of a clock.

Runs posting Passes quickly (in his triumph).

Jack of the clock A mechanical figure of a man, which is still to be seen in the clocks of some cathedrals, striking the hours and quarters on a bell.

holp . . . wits Music was believed to have a curative effect on madness.

strange brooch A rare and precious ornament.

cheapest . . . too dear Richard implies that his price has fallen. In addressing him as 'royal', the groom has given Richard the opportunity to pun on 'royal', meaning a coin, worth ten groats more than a 'noble' – the name of another coin. The King is now worth no more than his 'noble' equal (peer) – the groom.

ern'd Grieved.
roan Of variegated colours.
clapping Patting.
gall'd Chafed, made sore.
jauncing Prancing, or being made to prance by.
art wont As is your custom. Presumably to prove the food was not
  poisoned.
rude Violent.
yields Provides.
thy seat Richard mounts to the 'heavenly throne'.
the rest i.e. the remaining dead bodies.

Act V Scene 6

King Henry, in Windsor Castle, receives news of rebellion in
Cirencester and of the executions of various conspirators –
including the Abbot of Westminster. The Bishop of Carlisle,
however, is permitted to live because of the 'high sparks of
honour' which his life has shown.

The King hears of the death of Richard from Exton, who
enters with Richard's body in a coffin. Bolingbroke is not grateful to Exton, and with a heavy conscience contemplates a voyage
to the Holy Land 'to wash this blood off from my guilty hand'.

Commentary

Bolingbroke hears of rebels who have burned Cirencester and is
also informed of the elimination of the leading conspirators who
threatened him. Laconically, he thanks the bearers of these
tidings. The mood is sombre. Henry IV reign has begun with
fire and bloodshed. Bolingbroke's mercy to the Bishop of Carlisle is generous. Exton's arrival with the body of Richard in a
coffin inspires no thanks from the King: grimly, he admits that
he wished him dead, but the cares of kingship are already very
apparent. The play ends mournfully; there is a sense of gathering darkness. The King is guilt-ridden. The high hopes manifest in his coronation have melted away. Colour has vanished
from the play, and the audience is left anticipating fulfilment of
the dire prophecies of Richard and Carlisle.

Ciceter Cirencester.
state Now used in the modern sense of 'nation-state'.
At large discoursed Related in detail.
clog Burdened (with conscience).

reverend room An obscure phrase. It may mean 'some position appropriate to your reverence'; or, some place of religious retreat, e.g. a monastery; alternatively it may be an ironical reference to a prison cell! One of the first two possibilities seem the most likely.

more than thou hast Presumably Carlisle has been confined in prison.

wrought Performed.

Cain A reference to the doom of Cain, the first murderer, who killed his brother, Abel. Cain was doomed to wander the earth – never finding rest.

incontinent Immediately.

Revision Questions on Act V

1 What light does the leave-taking of Richard and his Queen shed upon their relationship?

2 Comment on Northumberland's intervention in Scene 1. What is the dramatic effect of Richard's prophetic words to him?

3 Contrast the crowd's reception of Bolingbroke with that it gives to Richard. How do the descriptions which York gives affect you?

4 How do you react towards York's treatment of his son? Can it be justified?

5 Outline King Henry's complaints about his son.

6 Some critics think that Act V, Scene 3 is one of the worst scenes that Shakespeare ever wrote. What is your view? Your answer should involve some consideration of why such an adverse criticism might have been made.

7 Do you discern any change in Richard in Act V, Scene 5?

8 Discuss the significance of the Groom and the Keeper.

9 Comment on King Henry's treatment of a) Northumberland; b) Carlisle; c) Exton.

10 Discuss the reaction of Bolingbroke to the death of Richard.

Shakespeare's art in *Richard II*

The characters

Richard

The face that faced so many follies,
And was at last out-faced by Bolingbroke

Shakespeare's presentation of Richard in the opening scene of the play suggests that the King is in command of the difficult situation which confronts him. Faced with his bitterly antagonistic subjects, his manner is regal

Then call them to our presence; face to face,
And frowning brow to brow, ourselves will hear
The accuser and the accused freely speak.

Richard's failure to make peace between Bolingbroke and Mowbray is sometimes seen as an indication of his weakness and the contempt in which he is held by the powerful adversaries. This is perhaps unfair: it was his duty, according to the rules of challenge, to endeavour to patch up the quarrel without bloodshed. Equally, it was an acknowledged option of the antagonists to refuse to make peace. In any case, Richard maintains his grip on proceedings, when he authoritatively demands the presence of the rivals at Coventry: 'We were not born to sue, but to command.'

Gaunt, who is established early in the play as the voice of truth, first provides us with a less admirable portrait of the King. In his refusal to take up arms against the King, despite the pleas of the distraught widow of Gloucester, he nonetheless acknowledges that Richard has been implicated in Gloucester's murder. Historians generally agree that Richard was the instigator of the murder: Gloucester was killed in Calais, whilst he was held in captivity by Mowbray. Later in the play we are told that Aumerle, acting as the King's agent, in fact plotted the deed.

Armed with this supposition, we may approach the King's performance at Coventry with greater insight than was possible hitherto. Once again, the manner is regal. Trumpets sound and the pageantry of the tournament proceeds. Richard's sudden intervention appears perhaps to be an example of caprice, and his later decision to alter the terms of Bolingbroke's banishment (whilst not similarly commuting Mowbray's sentence), has sometimes been seen as a mere whim. It is more attractive, in the light of Richard's probable involvement in Gloucester's death, to see a more Machiavellian motive at work. Mowbray cannot be allowed to win against Bolingbroke because he knows that the King has Gloucester's blood on his hands – and he may one day betray his knowledge. Perpetual banishment rids the King of this potential threat. Furthermore, there is some evidence in the play that Bolingbroke is becoming too popular for Richard's liking, and may be nourishing ambitious thoughts. Banishment again eradicates the threat: a rival is effectively disposed of. The reduction of the term for Bolingbroke may be a tacit acknowledgement of the popularity which Bolingbroke enjoys – in any case, Richard cannot lose by gaining a reputation for magnanimity, whilst still enforcing his basic wish. All this is suspicion rather than fact; Shakespeare as yet gives no clear indication as to how we should assess Richard.

Our doubts about the King are resolved in the next scene. Here we find him in the company of his favourites: Aumerle, Bagot and Greene. The King states his envy and fear of Bolingbroke's popularity and proposes to embark on a campaign in Ireland, which he will finance by dubious means – including farming out 'our realm' to the highest bidder. Off duty, as it were, the King comes across as essentially a malicious, misguided wastrel of the country's good.

The scene in which the dying Gaunt laments the fate of 'this blessed plot', and hopes to give some counsel to the King's 'unstaid youth', establishes finally the profundity of the kingdom's woes under such a shameful monarch:

A thousand flatterers sit within thy crown,
Whose compass is no bigger than thy head,
And yet, incaged in so small a verge,
The waste is no whit lesser than thy land.

Richard's response to Gaunt's solemn denunciation of him is insulting and trivial. York, who adds his voice to the condemnation which his brother has just uttered, receives blank incomprehension from the King: 'Why, uncle, what's the matter?' On the death of Gaunt, Richard alienates himself from us still further by confiscating the 'royalties and rights of banish'd Herford', which he by right should have inherited from his father. In abrogating these rights of inheritance, Richard undermines those very 'customary rights' whereby he came to the throne. In pointing out the heinousness of Richard's action, York is unequivocal:

Let not to-morrow then ensue today:
Be not thyself. For how art thou a king
But by fair sequence and succession?

Thus Shakespeare has established Richard as a bad king, whose
presence on the throne spells ruination for the country. It is not
surprising that a rebellion is soon afoot. Whilst Richard is pursuing his campaign in Ireland, Bolingbroke raises an army and
returns to claim his inheritance. This act of defiance towards the
banishment which the King had imposed has important implications. Gaunt had refused to 'stir' against the King in vengeance for Gloucester's death:

God's is the quarrel – for God's substitute,
His deputy anointed in His sight,
Hath caused his death; the which if wrongfully,
Let heaven revenge, for I may never lift
An angry arm against His minister.

Richard may be a bad king, but he reigns by Divine sanction, and
to rebel against him represents an act of sacrilege.

When Richard lands at Barkloughly, he greets England and in
an emotional vein proclaims his confidence in Divine protection.
He believes that:

God for his Richard hath in heavenly pay
A glorious angel: then, if angels fight,
Weak men must fall, for heaven still guards the right.

This confidence is soon shattered by the information which he
receives in the course of the scene, and Richard's faith in his
inviolability gives way to despair: it would appear that God has
deserted him. He only looks forward to death. He disbands his
army. As his material strength diminishes, however, so we find
ourselves taking up a new attitude towards Richard. Previously
there had been much to despise in him and much which seems
to justify Bolingbroke's rebellion, but as he struggles to come to
terms with his loss of power, so we begin to sympathize with his
predicament and the suffering that it induces.

By the time that he is confronted by Bolingbroke at Flint
Castle, Richard has recovered himself sufficiently to make a
ringing assertion of his kingly authority. To Northumberland he
says:

Tell Bolingbroke, for yon methinks he stands,
That every stride he makes upon my land
Is dangerous treason.

But once Bolingbroke has made his demands, and acting on the advice of Aumerle, Richard finds that 'gentle words' are probably the best course open to him. The realization that he must placate his subjects brings home to him the reality of his situation. He is no longer a king to command. In a touching speech Richard shows us that he understands that he must now lose everything:

What must the king do now? Must be submit?
The king shall do it. Must he be deposed?
The king shall be contented. Must he lose
The name of king? a God's name, let it go.

At this point, he launches into a highly metaphorical speech in which he envisages himself leading the life of a hermit and eventually finding 'an obscure grave'. Aumerle weeps. Undeterred, he continues and imagines that their combined tears will 'fret' us 'a pair of graves'. It is not long before he has handed over his realm to 'King Bolinbroke'.

Richard's behaviour at this point has disappointed some critics and they have drawn attention to his self-pity, his whimsicality and his instability. Richard is probably guilty of all charges. But it seems that Shakespeare is concerned with more than simply showing us Richard wallowing in his own sense of loss. It may be self-indulgent to engage in a number of elaborate conceits at this time of crisis, but it is a way of coming to terms with the situation – and there is nothing else at this stage that Richard can do. His faith in 'the divinity that doth hedge a king' has been destroyed, and his very identity, which has always hitherto depended upon the knowledge that he is King, has apparently vanished. No longer sure who he is, Richard seeks retirement and death. Bolingbroke, in the ascendant, has other ideas: the King must go to London.

In Act IV, Scene 1 Richard formally abdicates. It is obvious that the episode has been carefully arranged by Bolingbroke: Richard is to declare his follies in public and to hand over the crown. In the speech in which Richard says that he intends to 'undo' himself, we sense a water-shed in the play. Richard's struggle and suffering have centred on his attempt to come to terms with the loss of kingship. Grief at the loss has been the predominant emotion, and it has been grief expressed with such poetic power that it can hardly have failed to move us to pity. As Richard performs his 'inverted coronation', we become aware of a dignity about him, which derives partly from the rhetorical formality of his words. If the metaphor of 'the play' may be invoked: Bolingbroke thought that he was the director of the piece, but at this point it is Richard who is speaking his own lines – *not* Bolingbroke's. Thus, what might appear to be an act of surrender is, in fact, an act of assertion. The calm dignity with which Richard speaks tells us that he is in control of himself (and his mute audience). He has come to terms with what he is doing: handing over the crown. It is his moment.

Significantly, Richard asserts himself again soon afterwards when he refuses to denounce himself publicly. He scorns the bullying Northumberland:

Nay, if I turn mine eyes upon myself,
I find myself a traitor with the rest.

There is yet another key-moment to come. Taking everybody by surprise, Richard calls for a mirror and regards himself in it. For a few brief moments he speaks of what he sees. It is as if he compresses into the image of himself all that being a king meant to him. It recalls his flatterers, his former power to command 'ten thousand men', the sacred radiance of a 'sun-king'. It also reminds him, of course, of his own physical beauty. In a fit of anguish, Richard dashes the mirror to the ground. Thus the episode becomes an emblem of the vanity and fragility of all that Richard held dear. As he continued to stare at his reflection he became aware that

A brittle glory shineth in this face;
As brittle as the glory is the face.

At this moment, what he sees and the truth are at variance: the glory of the face does not match what he feels within. He no longer has any connection with 'glory', and the glory of his face is a reminder of what he has lost. In the act of smashing the mirror, he destroys the painful image of what he has been.

Alone and deprived of everything, Richard comes to a final confrontation of himself at Pomfret Castle – in a prison cell his glories have sunk to this. Again in despair, he sees himself as a mere automaton– acting out the commands of Bolingbroke. His attempt to 'hammer out' some solace for his condition fails: he cannot play the beggar, nor the king – there seems no place for him. In response to the ill-played music, he blesses the musician who loves him enough to play for him. His manner with the Groom who comes to pay his respects is kindly and loving:

Rode he on Barbary? Tell me gentle friend,
How went he under him?

In his final moments he finds the strength to fight with his assailants. These episodes, just before he dies, together with his moment of self-recognition: 'I wasted time, and now doth time waste me' all contribute to the high pathos of Richard's death. He dies showing some of his most sympathetic characteristics.

But to stress too much the 'heroic' moments which surround Richard's death would be to distort, in the interests of neatness, the central dilemma of the play. We should not fall into the trap of 'forgiving' Richard and investing him with a glory, which correspondingly blackens Bolingbroke. Richard was not, and never could have, made a good king. To the last we see evidence of his self-centredness: he feels affronted that his horse should bear Bolingbroke 'so proud'. His final words are of his ascent to heaven. Throughout the play we have been made aware of his grief at the loss of majesty. Richard's 'self' has been constantly and vividly laid before us – by Richard. It has been left to others to think of the good of England: notably Gaunt and Carlisle. In concentrating with great intensity on his own agonies, Richard has largely ignored larger issues. Except for the musician and the Groom, Richard scarcely seems to care for anybody but himself. Thus the dilemma: Richard is God's anointed king, but he is plainly unfit to govern; Bolingbroke is the usurper, but seems eminently suited to rule. Richard's character exemplifies the dangers inherent when the principle of the 'Divine Right of Kings' is embodied in human frailty.

The story of Richard, as presented by Shakespeare, enacts a tragic sequence of events. We are witnesses to the decline and fall of Richard from a position of eminence to the moment when he dies. The first part of the play establishes that this fall is due in large measure to faults in Richard's character, which render him unsuited to the role which fate has called upon him to play. There is also a feeling that, struggle as he may, Bolingbroke will inevitably defeat him – and the fact is that Richard does not really struggle at all. Any luck that is available always seems to favour Bolingbroke: the Welsh opposition evaporates, Richard happens to be in Flint Castle.

In response to the circumstances which confront him, Richard cannot seem to summon the will to fight, but far from alienating us from him, Shakespeare chooses to engage our sympathies for the stricken King. This he does partly by the use of ancillary characters such as the Queen, and partly by giving Richard hauntingly beautiful speeches, which yield us unforgettable insights into his situation and his suffering. Thus we empathize with Richard in his fall, whilst still acknowledging that he is not suited for kingship.

In our examination of the death of Richard, we have seen that in the end he came to realize that he was to blame for his loss of the crown. Also he was shown as capable of appreciating humble characters, something he did not manifest whilst he was King. He also discovered the will to fight his assailants. Shakespeare has thus presented him at his height, just before he dies. Richard has learned from what has happened to him, but it is too late for him to put what he has learned to any good effect. As Richard's body is brought before Bolingbroke, we find that we are, perhaps, prepared to lament his passing, in a way that would have been impossible for us at an earlier stage in the play.

It will be apparent from our survey of Richard that Shakespeare portrays him as a character whose moods fluctuate. Our attitude towards him is correspondingly variable. He begins regally (at Coventry, for example), but he can be maliciously frivolous (with Gaunt, for example). He is prepared to farm out the realm, yet when he returns from Ireland he speaks of England in terms of the deepest affection: 'Dear earth, I do salute thee with my hand'. He faces the insults of the crowd with patient dignity, 'His face still combating with tears and smiles'; yet at times he can indulge in morbid self-pity. At the end, he even manages to summon the courage to fight his assailants.

Two points, perhaps, need to be made when we come to consider Richard as a whole. First, he is almost entirely self-centred: his thoughts and actions are devoted to exploring his own reactions and feelings. He hears of the deaths of his friends Bushy, Greene and Wiltshire – and this immediately prompts a long, introspective consideration of himself:

For God's sake, let us sit upon the ground,
And tell sad stories of the death of kings.

The significant thing here is not so much that he talks about the prospect of the death of kings, but more that he does not give one thought to his former friends. Related to this aspect of his character, is his tendency to see what is happening to him as if he were an actor in a drama. At Coventry, he played the king; as Bolingbroke strips power from him he plays the role of the deposed monarch – in so doing, he actually anticipates his abdication, even before he meets with the victorious Bolingbroke:

By heaven, I'll hate him everlastingly
That bids me be of comfort, any more.

Go to Flint Castle: there I'll pine away;
A king, woe's slave, shall kingly woe obey.

To play his part, he finds the most hauntingly beautiful words; to express his feelings he finds the most evocative conceits. Imprisoned, he talks of populating his cell with thoughts:

And these same thoughts people this little world
In humours like the people of this world.

In a sense, this is what he has often done throughout the play. We have seen the play 'peopled' by Richard's thoughts – and he has played the leading role.

By creating this Richard, Shakespeare has put before us an insight into the nature of being a king. Kings inevitably are both men, and they are kings – men , who are invested with the role of 'God's substitute', and with this role go the various appurtenances of power. Richard may be seen 'playing the king' at the outset, but he does not embrace the responsibilities which go with 'the part': he enjoys the ceremony, but as 'God's substitute' he is a failure. Bolingbroke seizes his chance and Richard has to change his performance to that of grieving, deposed king. He plays his part from his heart – and we are moved to tears.

Henry Bolingbroke

How high a pitch his resolution soars!

There can be no doubt about Bolingbroke's achievement in the play, but his character and motivations are enigmatic. He bursts on the scene with great force, demanding vengeance for Gloucester's death and accusing Mowbray of the crime. Despite Richard's concern that the matter be dropped, he refuses – thus defying the wishes of his King and father. He proclaims that it is a matter of honour, and Richard agrees to his wishes. At Coventry, when Richard puts a stop to the tournament and banishes him, he accepts the King's judgment – harsh though it is – with few words ('Your will be done') and later he acknowledges 'such is the breath of kings'. He receives no comfort from his father's attempt to cheer him as he goes into banishment: in a dignified and tender farewell he leaves England:

Where'er I wander boast of this I can,
Though banish'd, yet a true-born Englishman.

We cannot doubt Bolingbroke's forcefulness; his strength is

apparent in his acceptance of adversity; his patriotism and sense of honour are not in doubt.

When Bolingbroke raises an army and returns to England we are told that he comes merely to seek restoration of the dukedom which Richard confiscated on the death of his father. With typical directness he claims: 'It must be granted that I am Duke of Lancaster.' Doubts about his true motives are raised, however, when he proceeds to deal out punishment to the King's favourites. In a sense, it is true that they have been accessories to the King's injustice against him, but it does seem that he is exceeding his avowed aim in dispatching Bushy, Greene and other friends of the King's.

Richard, himself, is in no doubt: Bolingbroke's actions denote treason, and, although Bolingbroke pronounces that he intends to be 'yielding water' to the King's fire, when matters come to a head at Flint Castle, in accepting the King's surrender, it is nonetheless Bolingbroke who is clearly in charge:

Rich. For do we must what force will have us do.
         Set on towards London, cousin, is it so?
Bol.   Yea, my good lord.

It is not necessary for Bolingbroke to plot, nor even to mount a serious military campaign against Richard, for the King simply gives in, in the face of superior forces. Bolingbroke does not make any pronouncements about his ambitions – the throne is left vacant and he takes it. The only suggestions that he may be ambitious come from York and Richard:

York. Take not, good cousin, further than you should,
         Lest you mistake: the heavens are o'er our heads.

and

Rich. What says King Bolingbroke? Will his Majesty
         Give Richard leave to live till Richard die?

The silence with which Bolingbroke answers these remarks on his long-term aims, can only cast doubt on his integrity.

In the scene in Westminster Hall (IV,1), Bolingbroke manages competently a difficult and ugly situation, as the war of words between Aumerle and his adversaries threatens to get out of hand. In contrast to Richard, when he dealt with Bolingbroke and Mowbray, Bolingbroke, in this instance, says relatively little. This may be interpreted as an inability to take charge, but equally it could be argued that he lets the storm blow itself out and then he intervenes. The doubt is there: is it lack of control, or is it shrewd policy? The fact is that when he does speak he is crisp and decisive – and he is listened to.

When Bolingbroke is offered, and accepts, the throne, his reticence is again note-worthy and enigmatic. In direct contrast to Richard, who can never resist the opportunity to 'unpack his heart with words', Bolingbroke merely says: 'In God's name, I'll ascend the throne.' Carlisle's outburst at this point elicits no response. From Bolingbroke's silence we may deduce a host of things. Is he feeling guilty? Is he ignoring the charges? We cannot tell for certain. It is attractive to believe that the charges do go home. In permitting Northumberland to arrest Carlisle, he neatly avoids having to order it himself and thus, perhaps, avoids appearing overtly dictatorial, which might be bad policy at this juncture. His first act as King is thus *not* personally to order the arrest of his first critic.

Bolingbroke often seems to use Northumberland to perform the awkward tasks, which might threaten his popularity, or in any way show him in a dubious light. Similarly, he stops Northumberland from bullying Richard into a public confession of his crimes. It may be simple magnanimity, but the suspicion is that it suits him politically to appear merciful at this stage. Because he tells us so little about himself, we are free to put our own interpretation on almost everything he does. It is a certainty that he does not put a foot wrong, whatever his motives.

In the final scene, it becomes apparent that the mopping-up of the opposition has been effectively carried out. He has already pardoned Aumerle, now he pardons Carlisle – giving as his reason the 'high sparks of honour' that the Bishop has shown. Another magnanimous gesture, but we never warm to Bolingbroke. He clearly possesses the qualities which Richard lacked: he is authoritative, efficient, direct and he is popular with the masses. But he is colourless beside Richard. We would wish for some evidence of human feeling. Perhaps we find it at the end. Since his return from exile, Bolingbroke has not had to struggle for the throne – it has fallen his way and he has picked it up. He has, however, had to listen to others (Carlisle, for example) pointing out the implications of what was happening, and he has also listened to dire prophecies of what is to come. For the most part, he has remained silent or non-committal about what he has heard. But when he learns of the death of Richard, we hear him speak about his inner feelings, and we learn of his guilt at what has been done. He is never more human than at this moment:

Lords, I protest my soul is full of woe
That blood should sprinkle to make me grow.
Come mourn with me for what I do lament,
And put on sullen black incontinent.
I'll make a voyage to the Holy Land,
To wash this blood off from my guilty hand.

John of Gaunt

O, but they say the tongues of dying men
Enforce attention like deep harmony

Gaunt, who has a clear appreciation of Richard's faults and
follies, nonetheless refuses to entertain the idea that he should
rebel against him. He accepts the banishment of his son and
refuses to avenge his brother's murder. He is a staunch believer
in the Divine Right of Kings, and patriotism is his prime motiva-
tion. Above all personal considerations Gaunt puts the good of
the country, and for this reason, he is constantly critical of
Richard. Sensing that he is about to die, he calls the King to him
in the hope that he may 'breathe some counsel to his unstaid
youth'. His speech conjures up a glowing picture of England
('This royal throne of kings, this scept'red isle . . .'), which has
been betrayed ('made a shameful conquest of itself') by Richard.

We are reminded, notably by the Duchess of Gloucester, that
Gaunt is the son of Edward III, and , as such, his values hark
back to a bygone golden age, against which Richard's times are
judged, and found to be wanting. Richard is heedless and contemptuous of what Gaunt stands for, and he openly mocks the
dying old man. But Henry Bolingbroke, too, ignores the values
which his father represents when he decides to 'lift an angry
arm' and rebel against Richard 'God's substitute, His deputy
anointed in his sight'. It is an article of faith for Gaunt that only
God has the right to judge the King.

Northumberland

thou ladder wherewithal
The mounting Bolingbroke ascends my throne

Northumberland is involved with Bolingbroke's rebellion at an
early stage and he remains by his side throughout his rise to
power. As a man, Northumberland is brisk and down-to-earth.
His main motive for joining the faction would seem to be hatred
of the flatterers, with whom Richard surrounds himself. North-

umberland would no doubt be delighted to be ordered to see to the 'dispatch' of Bushy and Greene. Northumberland informs the King that Bolingbroke's ambition extends no further than the restoration of the dukedom of Lancaster, but his sincerity is in doubt in view of his low opinion of Richard. It is plain that Northumberland has little patience with Richard, and he shows a marked lack of sympathy with the suffering monarch:

> Sorrow and grief of heart
> Makes him speak fondly like a frantic man.

So much for Richard's delicate conceits on tears and graves! Northumberland is also apparently unmoved by the solemn denunciation which Carlisle utters in Act IV, Scene 1:

> Well have you argued, sir, and, for your pains,
> Of capital treason we arrest you here.

Callously, too, he is insistent that the King reads out the 'articles' which catalogue Richard's 'grievous crimes'. We may also find unsympathetic his separation of Richard and his Queen, as they say farewell in Act V, Scene 1. He is unmoved by Richard's strictures on his guilt:

> My guilt be on my head, and there an end.
> Take your leave and part, for you must part forthwith.

Bolingbroke finds the blunt, insensitive Northumberland useful. Apart from his practical help, he enables Bolingbroke to be merciful – to Richard over the reading of the articles, and to Carlisle. But he is especially useful in his ability to handle the practicalities attendant upon the rebellion: he initiates the support for Bolingbroke before he arrives in England, and he eliminates King Henry's enemies once he is on the throne. Of course, there may ultimately be dangers for Bolingbroke from such a man as Northumberland.

The Duke of York

I do remain as neuter

The Duke of York possesses the same instincts as his brother, John of Gaunt – but he has a different temperament and he faces different circumstances. Although he agrees with Gaunt that Richard has betrayed his office, he urges that Gaunt deals 'mildly' with his 'giddy youth', and, after Gaunt has spoken, he tries to smooth the King's ruffled feathers. On the death of Gaunt, however, it is a measure of the outrage which he feels about the confiscation of his lands, that even York is moved to rebuke the King in round terms: 'How long shall I be patient? . . .'

York is left in charge of the realm whilst Richard is in Ireland and is therefore called upon to face the threat of Bolingbroke. He is clearly out of his depth; his forces are weak. Nonetheless he denounces Bolingbroke. His defiance is short-lived and he throws in his lot with the rebels, accepting the assurance that Bolingbroke comes 'but for his own'.

For the rest of the play he is loyal to Bolingbroke – despite a lingering respect for Richard, which surfaces from time to time. It is York who offers Bolingbroke the Crown. York's difficult position is emphasized when he has to denounce his own son, because he cannot bring himself to break his oath of loyalty to Bolingbroke.

The overall impression of York is that he is an old man who is simply not able to cope with the crisis which arises as a result of the rebellion. He opts for the relatively quiet subordinate role which collaboration offers him.

The Bishop of Carlisle

High sparks of honour in thee have I seen

Carlisle is a man of principle and his loyalty to Richard never wavers. When Richard is confronted by the rebellious Bolingbroke in Wales, Carlisle is adamant that the King should fight and not abjectly surrender:

Fear and be slain – no worse can come to fight;
And fight and die is death destroying death.

His earlier advice, to the effect that 'Heaven helps those who help themselves', reveals that he is not an unworldly churchman.

The clearest statement which Carlisle makes of his beliefs occurs in Act IV, Scene 1. Bolingbroke asserts that he will 'in God's name' ascend the regal throne. This is too much for Carlisle: brusquely, and courageously, he speaks out:

Marry, God forbid!
Worst in this royal presence may I speak,
Yet best beseeming me to speak the truth.

The words which follow establish a clear moral framework whereby Bolingbroke's assumption of regality may be judged: a subject has no right to 'give sentence on his king', for the King is 'the figure of God's majesty' and to so judge him is a 'heinous, black, obscene deed'. Carlisle is thus an unflinching believer in the Divine Right of the King to rule. The dire prophecy for the future of England, if the 'traitor' Bolingbroke is permitted to have his way, when 'future ages groan for this foul act' – has the ring of conviction, and, as Shakespeare's audience would realize did, in fact, come to pass.

Carlisle is involved in the plot to overthrow Henry IV; unlike York, he is always ready to stand up for what he believes. To his credit, Bolingbroke forgives him and he is permitted to 'choose out some secret place' where he may 'joy thy life'.

Aumerle

My transgressing boy

Aumerle, son of the Duke of York, is one of the King's supporters. His jests, which trivialize the solemn moment of Bolingbroke's departure into exile, do not create a good first impression (Act I, Scene 4). When it becomes clear that Richard has been out-manoeuvred by Bolingbroke, he nonetheless stands by the King and endeavours to cheer his fading spirits. Aumerle's advice to Richard at Flint Castle is shrewdly practical:

> let's fight with gentle words,
> Till time lend friends, and friends their helpful swords.

Unfortunately, by this time Richard is unable to appreciate the sensible advice he is given – he ignores Aumerle.

Richard's fortunes decline still further, but Aumerle sticks by him. He is denounced as the murderer of Gloucester: a charge which he courageously denies.

Aumerle's loyalty to Richard is further exemplified when he joins the plot to overthrow Bolingbroke. Once this is discovered by his father, who proposes to betray him, he agrees with his mother that he should throw himself on Bolingbroke's mercy and seek a pardon. Clearly Aumerle's adherence to Richard's cause does have its limits: he will take risks for him, but he will not die for him. Bolingbroke does pardon him, and Shakespeare records that he dies nobly on the field of Agincourt in the play *Henry V*.

The Queen

Rue, even for ruth, here shortly shall be seen,
In remembrance of a weeping queen.

There can be no doubt that the Queen loves Richard. We sense this particularly in the anguish which she feels when she learns from the Gardener of her husband's overthrow. As she waits for Richard to pass by on his way to the Tower, she represents a picture of helpless suffering, but it is noticeable that she possesses enough spirit to attempt to shake him from his reverie of an after-life together – she is more concerned with the here and now:

What! is my Richard both in shape and mind
Transform'd and weakened? Hath Bolingbroke
Depos'd thine intellect? Hath he been in thy heart?

But she is always the bystander at events, as is evidenced by the nameless dread she feels whilst her husband is in Ireland. As we watch the suffering which she undergoes, we cannot but find our feeling for Richard becoming altered: we begin to look for the qualities which can inspire such grief in a manifestly good and sensible woman. Thus the Queen contributes powerfully to the pathos which surrounds Richard and his circumstances.

Minor characters

Scroope He is loyal to Richard, and his chief function in the play is to be the bearer of bad tidings when Richard lands in North Wales.

Salisbury He endeavours to delay the dispersal of the King's Welsh forces. His news that they have, in fact, dispersed is particularly dispiriting to Richard. As a measure of his loyalty, he is executed by Bolingbroke.

Bushy, Bagot, Greene Virtually ciphers and indistinguishable. Bushy seeks to solace the grieving Queen. Bagot accuses Aumerle of Gloucester's murder. Bushy and Greene are executed by Bolingbroke because of their bad influence on the King.

Ross and Willoughby Because of Richard's behaviour towards Bolingbroke, they are prepared to join the rebels. The defection of these basically honest men is an indication of the heinousness of Richard's behaviour.

Duchess of Gloucester She fiercely demands that Gaunt should avenge the death of her husband. The scene in which she appears is important because it denotes Richard's criminality in ordering Gloucester's death. Her reminder to Gaunt of his father (Edward III) places the events of the play in a wider perspective.

Duchess of York One of her functions is simply to listen to her husband's description of Bolingbroke's progress through London, and the corresponding humiliation of Richard. Her defence of Aumerle shows the soundness of her maternal instincts, and she pleads his case before Bolingbroke. Some might find her vehemence comic – Bolingbroke appears to do so.

A background to the History Plays

According to orthodox medieval philosophers, God created the universe and everything in it. It was an ordered structure and God presided over His creation. Each constituent of this cosmos had a fixed rank, or value, and fulfilled a function according to the dictates of Divine Providence. The order of the universe was manifest in hierarchies: at the top of the 'pyramid' was the Creator, beneath came the Angels, next Man – and so on down the scale, until one reached the humblest forms of inanimate matter. Each broad hierarchy was thought to be sub-divided into other hierarchies, and the functioning of the whole was dependent upon the correct functioning of its parts.

In the beginning all Creation was harmonious: God reigned in Heaven, Man, ranked below the Angels, was Lord of the Earth. The whole proclaimed the glory of the Creator and was bound together by Love and Divine Law. Unfortunately, because of the misuse of free-will, the harmony between Man and God was broken – discord entered the World, as a result of Sin. Man, or a man, might regain his favoured position in the Divine Scheme by virtue of God's grace, but he had to be continually on his guard lest he sin again, by giving way to his 'lower', or bestial, self. The consequences of such a falling-off were manifestly horrendous, and affected not only the individual sinner but also had ramifications in the world around him. The more eminent in the hierarchy the sinner, the more profound the sin, and so the consequences were the more dire.

In the Histories Shakespeare deals with order on the political level. According to the belief of many, the nation corresponded on earth with the hierarchy in Heaven. The king occupied the chief position in the nation. He ruled the state by Divine Right – he was God's representative on earth. Occupying this eminent position gave the king responsibilities as well as privileges: it was his duty to uphold the 'king-becoming graces', which are defined by Malcolm in *Macbeth*:

. . . justice, verity, temperance, stableness,
Bounty, perseverance, mercy, lowliness,
Devotion, patience, courage, fortitude.

In return for the exercise of these virtues, he could expect the loyalty and love of his subjects. Of course, in the fallen state of the world, the ideal was not possible: sin was manifest in kings and their subjects. Discord was an ever-present threat; chaos was consequent upon the breakdown of order.

To overthrow and murder the anointed king was conceived as an act of sacrilege and invited the direst punishment from the Almighty. The usurper, inevitably, would come to experience Divine Justice and a nation could expect no peace until the will of God was re-established. In extreme circumstances, echoing the disorder on earth, the very fabric of the heavens might become disordered: strange eclipses, comets, tempests were often supposed to be manifestations of Divine displeasure.

Tudor historians believed that history demonstrated the workings of God's justice and His vengeance. The period from the reign of Richard II through to the death of Richard III, was thought to reveal the workings of Divine Providence. Richard II, a bad king, who did not practise the 'king-becoming graces', nevertheless was God's anointed ruler. Henry Bolingbroke, in deposing him, committed sacrilege, and, as a consequence was punished by inner turmoil and civil unrest. There was a brief respite under the rule of Henry V, but the whole country was plunged into the Wars of the Roses during the reign of Henry VI. Richard III, himself a regicide, purged the nation at Bosworth – in this way, Richard III was a manifestation of the wrath of God. Finally, God's Providence was reasserted by the accession of Henry Tudor – a 'rightful' successor – and greatness was restored to the kingdom. By this means, a neat, schematic and propogandist interpretation was given to the chaos and blood-letting subsequent upon the usurpation of Richard II.

Themes

Kingship

Richard is King of England by Divine Right. This idea is constantly stressed in the play, most notably by the Bishop of Carlisle and John of Gaunt. Carlisle, at the very moment that Bolingbroke ascends the throne, eloquently denounces his right to do so:

And shall the figure of God's majesty,
His captain, steward, deputy elect,
Anointed, crowned, planted many years,
Be judg'd by subject and inferior breath,
And he himself not present?

Carlisle also foresees the consequences of such a 'heinous, black, obscene' deed: 'Disorder, horror, fear and mutiny.'

John of Gaunt, early in the play, although he perceives the inadequacies of Richard as King, and has himself suffered as a result of Richard's wickedness, nonetheless refuses to 'lift an arm' against him. Any punishment which may be due to Richard must come from God. The implication is that no subject can take upon himself the right to usurp the throne: to do so is to risk the disorder and chaos of which we have heard Carlisle speak. To defy God's ordinance is to create a free-for-all, in which anyone can claim the right to be king. Thus, the king's divinely-sanctioned authority, even if he is a bad king, is the linchpin of order in the state.

Richard and the Divine Right

Although Richard's right to be on the throne cannot be questioned, it is clear that we see in him a king who has abused that privilege. He behaves irresponsibly; he makes mistakes which derive from a belief that, as monarch, he is subject to no law – not even God's Law. Significantly, from the point of view of the theme of the play, he overthrows the law of succession when he disinherits Bolingbroke. It is by the operation of this law that he is King.

Faced with Bolingbroke, Richard still believes that he can rely on Divine protection:

Not all the water in the rude rough sea
Can wash the balm off from an anointed king;
The breath of worldly men cannot depose
The deputy elected by the Lord;
For every man that Bolingbroke hath press'd
To lift shrewd steel against our golden crown,
God for his Richard hath in heavenly pay
A glorious angel: then if angels fight,
Weak men must fall, for heaven still guards the right.

In this belief he is both right and wrong. He is wrong in the sense that he has sacrificed his right to rely on Divine protection by his unjust confiscation of Bolingbroke's inheritance: this has weakened his position morally. He is wrong, too, because his belief implies that the 'power that made (him) king, hath power to keep (him) king, in spite of all' – and that he is not called upon to *do* anything to assert that power. Carlisle reminds him that:

The means that heaven yields must be imbrac'd
And not neglected; else, heaven would,
And we will not; heavens offer, we refuse
The proffered means of succour and redress.

However, Richard is right in the sense that, the balm cannot be washed off from God's anointed. In the deposition scene, he goes through what has been termed an 'inverted coronation':

With mine own tears I wash away my balm,
With mine own hands I give away the crown . . .

Here, Richard enacts a moving interlude, but the fact is that, try as he may, the balm is *not* washed away any more effectively by his tears, than it might be by 'the rough rude sea'. In his prison cell at Pomfret, momentarily, he wishes himself a beggar, but penury straightaway persuades him that 'I was better when a king'. The fact would seem to be that the Divine Right to be King can only be removed by God who gave it. This brings us back to Carlisle's defence of Richard before Bolingbroke – no man has the right to judge or sentence a king – not even, apparently, the King himself. As Gaunt put it: 'God's is the quarrel . . . let heaven revenge.' For Richard this means that he must continue until death to suffer the knowledge that he is God's King, without the wherewithal to be King.

Fit to govern – Bolingbroke

Shakespeare spends much of the early part of the play showing us that Richard is not fit to govern – we need not enumerate his faults yet again. Here we approach the central theme of the play: Bolingbroke manifestly *is* fit to govern. He may lack Richard's appeal as a human being, indeed, we learn very little of him as a person – but his competence to rule cannot be doubted. Shakespeare is careful to avoid blackening Henry Bolingbroke as a man, despite the fact that he is a usurper. He has considerable moral right to feel outraged by Richard's confiscation of his inheritance. We do not see him glorying in the glory which he achieves: as he rides through London after his coronation, despite the hero-worship of the crowd, his manner is dignified and humble:

Whilst he, from one side to the other turning,
Bare-headed, lower than his proud steed's neck,
Bespake them thus, 'I thank you, countrymen.'

He behaves magnanimously towards Richard over the reading of the public confession. He shows mercy to the Bishop of Carlisle. It may be argued that all this is evidence of a shrewd politician. True, there can be little doubt that Bolingbroke is interested in power, but there is not necessarily anything wrong with this, provided that we can believe that the power, once gained, will be properly used – and in Bolingbroke's case, there is much reason to suppose that he will be a strong and efficient ruler. The Gardener, one supposes, would find praiseworthy Bolingbroke's ability to 'prune' the country, and his desire to eliminate the caterpillars which have for so long infested the realm. In any case, we do not see Bolingbroke much engaged in actively pursuing power. He raises an army to redress his wrongs; after that, Richard virtually surrenders the crown and Bolingbroke accepts what is offered him.

Thus we have it: Richard, King by Divine Right, but unfit to rule; Bolingbroke, with many of the qualities of a king, but without the Divine sanction. As always, Shakespeare presents us with the issue, but we are left to make up our minds. The plays are dramas about people, with all their complexities and ambiguities, they are not history, neat parables, nor propaganda. If conclusions must be reached, we might begin with John of Gaunt's evocation of England in Act II, Scene 1. the 'demi-paradise' which he conjures before us is clearly absent under the kingship of Richard, and we can have little confidence that it will be present under Henry IV –

there are too many clouds on the horizon, and usurpation is a crime which must be paid for. For all his good fortune and strengths Bolingbroke begins his reign in sombre mood, promising to expiate his sin by a Crusade to the Holy Land. It is a promise which he is never able to keep, and the dire prophecies, which make such a powerful impact when they are spoken, all come true. Given his follies, it is ironical that Shakespeare should make us feel a sense of sadness at the passing of Richard, and a sense of foreboding now that Bolingbroke is King. The only certainty would seem to be that England is about to undergo a long period of suffering, as wilful men struggle for power. This play has examined the genesis of the turmoil, but it has not enabled us neatly to apportion the blame – both Richard and Bolingbroke have too much right – and too much wrong – on their sides.

Changing times

During the course of the play we witness the passing of an old order and the establishing of a new era. Particularly at the beginning of the play, there are numerous references to the time of Edward III. It is seen as a time when England was bathed in glory – triumphant abroad and harmonious at home. Richard is the son of the Prince of Wales, the heroic Black Prince:

In war was never lion rag'd more fierce,
In peace was never gentle lamb more mild,
Than was that young and princely gentleman.

It is of this past 'golden' age that Gaunt speaks, in his famous evocation of patriotic splendour: 'This blessed plot, this earth, this realm, this England.' But Gaunt soon dies, and his vision passes from view with him. York, the last of 'the seven vials' of Edward III's 'sacred blood', is old and ineffective

The 'real' world of the play is different. The Richard whom we see at the outset may have his father's fair outward appearance, but the inner man is vain, frivolous, irresponsible and a dreamer. England under his rule has been shamed. John of Gaunt's 'garden' of England is mis-managed. We may begin on a note of splendour and chivalry, but on the throne sits Richard, whose behaviour reveals scant respect for John of Gaunt, nor for his vision of England.

Into this world marches Bolingbroke. Initially, his behaviour at the tournament, and his desire to claim his just inheritance, show a respect for the past. But his actions involve the deposition of a king – and respect for the ancient Divine Right does not inhibit him from taking the throne when it is offered to him. Interestingly, Shakespeare does not show the taking of the throne to be an act of villainy; he studiously avoids painting Bolingbroke as a Machiavel. The process by which Bolingbroke becomes Henry IV is shown rather to be the inevitable consequence of circumstances – perceiving the strengths and weaknesses of both, Shakespeare does not apparently take sides between Bolingbroke and Richard.

But Divine Right gives way in the face of usurping force. Bolingbroke's shrewd management of his resources, and Richard's lack of resources and will, ensure that the transference of power is achieved with the minimum of fuss. The new order is established.

Deprived of material power, Richard can only fall back on evocations of old traditions and dreams of majesty, which he himself sees are ineffective to assert kingly authority. The play then moves into an elegaic mode, and Richard movingly and with great lyricism, laments 'the death of kings'. In a sense, it is an appropriate theme, for England under Bolingbroke will never know the peace and harmony of the former times. Thus the play ends on a sombre note, with the dire prophecies of Carlisle ringing in our ears. The King, weak in his inability to claim the Divine Right to underpin his kingship, will need to exercise all his political and military skills to remain secure on the throne – and it is a bad beginning, for he is weighed down by guilt.

We can sense in the play that, despite the many weaknesses of Richard as a king, with his passing departs the glory and majesty of a bygone age. This is Shakespeare's great achievement: he has managed to show us a Richard who is manifestly a bad ruler, supplanted by Bolingbroke who is manifestly a competent ruler – and yet we can still feel the momentousness and sadness of Richard's passing from the stage.

We may, perhaps, account for this feeling by reflecting on the new world which Bolingbroke brings with him. For all his weaknesses Richard is associated constantly in our minds with poetry, colour and the Divine sanction for rule, which can never be stripped from him by mortal hands – this has been the abiding tenor of the play after the King's return from Ireland. Richard's overthrow is portrayed as having disastrous consequences for England. Without taking sides between Bolingbroke and Richard, Shakespeare is unequivocally on the side of England, and deprived of the rightful King, a struggle for power between men is the inevitable consequence – order, divinely-ordained, is destroyed by man. Bolingbroke is self-reliant, and he brings with him a world in which self-reliance is at a premium. It is not a world to which we can give whole-hearted assent. Richard's ineffective dreams and poeticism give way to the workmanlike, and sometimes brutal tones of Bolingbroke and his associates, who are all practical and self-reliant men:

North. My guilt be on my head, and there an end. Take leave, and part; for you must part forthwith.
Queen. Banish us both, and send the king with me.
North. That were some love, but little policy.

Thus the world of Bolingbroke is the world of 'policy' and we cannot feel at home in it. With the old securities of tradition and love 'banished', we are left uncertain of our bearings. We may not approve of all we have seen of Richard, but at least our moral judgements were fairly clear. We are simply not sure about Bolingbroke, we never learn what sort of man he really is. All we can be sure of, as we enter this world in which actions are based on 'policy', is that it is likely to be every man for himself – brute strength will prevail. It is not surprising that the play ends ominously and not on a note of triumph:

March sadly after; grace my mournings here,
In weeping after this untimely bier.

Structure and style

Structure

The play has a remarkable unity because it focuses with such intensity upon the thoughts and feelings of Richard himself. His decline and death are balanced by the rise of Bolingbroke, the other main character, but, although their characters are sharply contrasted, we receive much less information about Bolingbroke's make-up than we receive about Richard's.

As a general proposition, it might be said that the dramatic conflict is carried on in 'debate' rather than action. As has been frequently pointed out, the plot, in comparison with the other History Plays, is relatively slight. Such opportunities for action as Shakespeare might have embraced (for example, Holinshed's description of Richard's ambush and capture in Wales), have been avoided.

The idea of the 'debate' is exemplified in many of the scenes. In the first scene Mowbray and Bolingbroke are engaged in a war of words – with the King in the middle. This scene relates to a parallel scene later in the play, when Aumerle is forced to defend himself in front of the new King at Westminster. In the same light, we might see the scene between Richard and Gaunt, Gaunt and the Duchess of Gloucester, Richard and Bolingbroke at Flint, York and his wife – to mention just a few. They are all scenes in which argument takes place, with varying degrees of vehemence. Richard's major speeches, although nominally spoken to people, sometimes seem to be soliloquies in which he tries to unravel in words the conflict between his status as King, and the realities of his loss of power.

The first scene, full of energy, captures our interest by plunging us into the bitter quarrel between Bolingbroke and Mowbray: our anticipation of the outcome at Coventry is intense. The scene at Coventry, with all its pageantry, is even more visually captivating than the initial court scene, but by this time Shakespeare has undermined what may be our favourable first impression of Richard by the insertion of the second scene, in which he is implicated in the Duke of York's murder. Our feelings about Richard are alienated still further by his behaviour with John of Gaunt and his confiscation of Bolingbroke's estates. Thus the first part of the play, with vividness and economy, and by showing us the public and the private Richard, has demonstrated the reasons why he deserves to lose his throne. It has also established that Richard is the Divinely-sanctioned monarch.

The next phase, which is initiated by the success of Boling-broke on his return from exile, shows us the transference of power. It all happens remarkably easily, but the scene with the Queen (II,2) prepares us to view Richard in a more sympathetic light. As power is taken from him, so we find that the King's plight engages our sympathies, whilst at the same time, Shakes-peare does not alienate us from Bolingbroke. The turning-point of the play occurs in this section of the action, when Richard disperses his forces (III,2). The King has lost, and from this scene onwards, his fate is determined. The 'set-piece' scene at Flint Castle is the climax of this part of the play because it brings King and rebel face-to-face – in the light of what has already been established in Act III Scene 2.

We are shown next several scenes which establish Richard's suffering and lead inexorably to the Deposition Scene, where the 'inverted coronation' puts the seal on Bolingbroke's rise to power.

The final phase shows us Bolingbroke securing the state, and, in the end, some partial recovery of spirit by the King – the tension of the suffering being released by his much-invoked death.

So much for the main outline of the play. There are various incidental scenes which underline the main processes and themes of the action, notably the 'Garden Scene' (III,4). Here, for a moment, we are allowed to stand back and contemplate, once again, the nature of Richard's kingship – just prior to the moment when he abdicates.

Style

The play is written predominantly in blank verse: unrhymed, alternately-stressed, ten-syllable lines. However, approximately one fifth of the play is in rhyme – mostly in couplets.

Variety

Bolingbroke tends to be given verse which is direct, spare and often imperious in manner:

Noble lord,
Go to the rude ribs of that ancient castle,

Through brazen trumpet send the breath of parle
Into his ruin'd ears, and thus deliver:
Henry Bolingbroke
On both his knees doth kiss King Richard's hand,
And sends allegiance and true faith of heart
To his most royal person

Often Bolingbroke confines himself to succinct remarks which convey the sense of a man of few words and of simple decisiveness: 'In God's name, I'll ascend the regal throne.' Sometimes, his laconic utterances come close in their rhythm to prose:

I thought you had been willing to resign.

Are you contented to resign the crown?

Richard, in contrast, is given to long speeches which are more blatantly 'poetical'. Such speeches reveal the King searching for conceits to enshrine his feelings:

for within the hollow crown
That rounds the mortal temples of a king
Keeps Death his court, and there the antic sits,
Scoffing his state and grinning at his pomp . . .
. . . and, humour'd thus,
Comes at last, and with a little pin
Bores through his castle wall, and farewell King!

At times, Richard can be highly rhetorical:

With mine own tears I wash away my balm,
With mine own hands I give away my crown,
With mine own tongue deny my sacred state . . .

Here the rhythm is akin to an incantation, and the speech as a whole is imbued with a sad formality. At other times, the elegaic note predominates:

In winter's tedious nights sit by the fire
With good old folks, and let them tell thee tales
Of woeful ages long ago betid;
And ere thou bid goodnight, to quite their griefs
Tell thou the lamentable tale of me,
And send the hearers weeping to their beds; . . .

It would be a mistake, however, to generalize. In Act II, for example, we find that Richard can adopt quite a different tone, when he speaks to Gaunt:

> A lunatic lean-witted fool,
> Presuming on an ague's privilege,
> Darest with thine frozen admonition
> Make pale our cheek, chasing the royal blood
> With fury from his native residence . . .
> Should run thy head from thy unreverent shoulders.

There is nothing very lyrical about this – the mocking, insensitive insults jar against the formality and dignity of the dying Gaunt. The clash of styles here vividly illustrates the gulf between sage adviser and irresponsible King. The contrast can sometimes be shocking: Richard's formality and regality at Coventry is brought down to earth by the jocularity of the scene which follows immediately upon it:

> *Rich.* We did observe. Cousin Aumerle,
> How far brought you high Herford on his way?
> *Aum* I brought high Herford, if you call him so,
> But to the next highway, and there I left him. (I,4)

The conversational tone and the ridicule apparent in this scene demonstrates, by means of the verse-style, the difference between the King's public and private persone.

Furthermore, on occasions, we find that Bolingbroke can indulge in conceit:

> Methinks King Richard and myself should meet
> With no less terror than the elements
> Of fire and water . . .
> The rage be his, whilst on earth I rain
> My waters – on the earth not him.

Word-play

The play abounds in puns and it is quite obvious that Shakespeare often enjoyed them simply for their own sake. Sometimes they strike the reader as frankly inapposite: it is difficult to reconcile Gaunt's lengthy puns on his own name (II, 1, 73–84) with his character and situation. Indeed, Richard remarks upon this very inconsistency: 'Can sick men play so nicely with their names?' And Gaunt's explanation for so doing does not carry conviction. Often, however, a pun can enhance our area of understanding. In the last example quoted above under variety there is a pun on 'rain' and 'reign'. In following up his own idea about himself being 'yielding water', it seems to occur naturally to Bolingbroke that he will be like 'rain' on earth. As he speaks this, it seems to develop into a sort of Freudian slip – which he immediately corrects ('on the earth not him'). But the pun has, perhaps, betrayed the reality of Bolingbroke's intentions, namely, that he intends to reign – both over the King and on earth. It is always worth examining each pun as it arises, and trying to decide if it is merely indulgence, or whether it sheds light on some area of the play's meaning.

Rhyme

There is often no apparent reason why Shakespeare suddenly has his characters speak in rhymed couplets. But explanations are sometimes available: rhymes, by tradition, denote the end of a scene. Rhyme, too, can give special force to a character's speech, making it stand out from the blank verse which surrounds it. The couplets which conclude York's warning to Richard in Act II, Scene 1, because of the rhyme, carry with them a proverbial force:

I'll not be by the while. My liege, farewell.
What will ensue hereof there's none can tell;
But by bad courses may be understood
That their events can never fall out good.

The artificiality of rhyme seems to fit well, when Bolingbroke is about to fight with Mowbray:

O, let no noble eye profane a tear
For me, if I be gor'd with Mowbray's spear
As confident as is the falcon's flight
Against a bird, do I with Mowbray fight.

The sureness of the strong rhymes conveys something of Bolingbroke's confidence as he goes to do battle – and the 'contrived' nature of the occasion creates a natural setting for such an unnatural mode of speech.

Finally, Shakespeare seems to enjoy slipping into rhyme in order to give some utterances a feeling of grace and flow – on these occasions there is an aesthetic pleasure to be had from the presence of rhyme: as Richard and the Queen part, their shared grief is suggested by the shared word-play and rhymes:

Rich.   Come, come, in wooing sorrow let's be brief,
        Since, wedding it, there's is such a length in grief:
        One kiss shall stop our mouths, and dumbly part;
        Thus give I mine, and thus take I thy heart.
Queen. Give me mine own again; twere no good part
        To take on me to keep and kill thy heart.
        So, now I have mine own again, be gone,
        That I may strive to kill it with a groan.

Imagery

We have already noted that Richard is prone to think of himself, and his situation as he loses the crown, in terms of conceits. A more detailed examination of these elaborate comparisons will reveal how Shakespeare employs them to give vividness and insight into the King's plight.

The full flow of imagery becomes apparent when the King returns from Ireland. He greets his country in terms of a child being reunited with its mother:

As a long-parted mother with her child
Plays fondly with her tears and smiles in meeting,
So weeping, smiling, greet I thee, my earth,
And do thee favours with my royal hands . . .

By this means the bond between King and realm is compared with one the most sacred of bonds which we can experience. Interestingly, this ties in with the idea that John of Gaunt had suggested when he described England as: 'This nurse, this teeming womb of royal kings.' It is relevant that both Gaunt and Richard speak of the relationship between King and realm in the same terms, because, of course, the inviolability of the relationship is one of the thematic ideas of the play.

Richard tends to see his suffering and degradation in religious terms

Did they not sometime cry 'All hail!' to me?
So Judas did to Christ. But he, in twelve,
Found truth in all but one; I, in twelve thousand, none.

As a comparison of course this will not strictly do – it comes close to blasphemy. But it is not blasphemous for the King to claim that, as God's substitute, his deposition and suffering may be likened to Christ's. The image thus gives an emotional colour to what is happening to Richard, which is both relevant to his character and to the Divine right theme of the play. In the same vein, the image of himself removing the sacred symbols of kingship ('sceptre', 'balm', 'crown' etc.) conveys the true nature of what is happening to him: the anointed king becoming a man. In fact, the play makes liberal use of religious imagery to indicate the way in which we should regard the events which are unfolding before us. Thus Carlisle can see the loss of the crown from the rightful king, as giving rise, in course of time, to an England which will be called 'The field of Golgotha and dead men's skulls'. In the same speech Carlisle also makes reference to the breaking of family ties in civil strife, which relates back again to the mother/child imagery of Gaunt and Richard.

There is also a strain of 'nature' imagery in the play. This is exemplified again by reference to Gaunt's famous 'England' speech. The country is 'this blessed plot'; Richard's favourites are an infestation of 'caterpillars'; it will soon become Carlisle's 'field of Golgotha'. The effect of this train of imagery is to suggest the betrayal and desecration of the ancient ideal which Gaunt visualizes in the most vivid, even apocalyptic terms.

It is a mammoth task to enumerate all the images which permeate the play. A few more examples will have to suffice. The Sun is an emblem of royalty: Richard, on his return, sees himself as the rising sun, banishing the night of Bolingbroke; to Bolingbroke Richard is 'the blushing discontented sun'; Salisbury sees Richard in terms of a setting sun 'weeping slowly in the west' (II, 4). The imagery suggests the decline of majesty.

Imagery of the ill-managed garden from Gaunt, the Gardeners and Bolingbroke is a powerful symbol of neglect and is reinforced by the suggestion that England has become 'a pelting farm'.

Richard is described by the Duchess as an unregarded actor (V, 2,33), an image which capture exactly some of the feelings which have been aroused by his behaviour during the course of the play. Indeed, in Act V Scene 5, Richard refers to himself in precisely these terms:

Thus play I in one person many people,
And none contented.

Finally, there is a single image which is thrown off by that master of the conceit, Richard himself, which seems to encapsulate with particular force and ingenuity the respective careers of the two main characters:

Now is this golden crown like a deep well
That owes two buckets, filling one another,
The emptier ever dancing in the air,
The other down, unseen and full of water:
That bucket down, and full of tears am I,
Drinking my griefs, whilst you mount up on high.

General questions

Note style answer

1 'Because, as a man, towards the end of the play Richard is a "sympathetic" figure, it is easy to miss the damning clarity with which, in the earlier part of the play, Shakespeare exposes his disastrous inadequacy as a king.' Discuss.

(a) *Consider* means, if any, whereby Shakespeare establishes Richard's inadequacy:
–Gaunt/York directly refer to personal failings
–Richard's behaviour/tone on hearing of Bolingbroke's departure (he's with his favourites).
–Richard's actions: kingdom farm'd out
                   implicated in Gloucester's murder.
  Does all this amount to damning clarity?
  Can you think of any more failings?
  Are there any 'plus points' for Richard? What about his handling of Bolingbroke and Mowbray – political shrewdness, or showy caprice?
  What weight would you give to Richard's confiscation of Gaunt's estates?
  Possible conclusion: all this does exemplify Richard's weaknesses with 'damning clarity'. He is shown to be personally irresponsible, from which derives his irresponsibilty as King.

(b) *Do you consider* that he is a sympathetic figure at the end of the play? If so, why?
What is the effect of:
–The Queen's grief for Richard?
–The fact that we are allowed into Richard's innermost thoughts and feelings, but not those of Bolingbroke?
–The manifest 'coldness' of Bolingbroke, and the insensitivity of his associate Northumberland?
–Richard's Divine Right to be King?
–The fight Richard puts up before he is killed?
–Richard's acknowledgement of his folly?
–The dire warnings of Carlisle?
–The poetic beauty with which he expresses his sufferings?
Possible conclusion: we are led to feel personally sympathetic towards Richard. Whilst we may feel antipathetic about his self-

pity, he does manage, by the end, to achieve a stature which he lacked at the beginning.

(c) *A problem*: has Shakespeare created a consistent character? Or, are there not two separate Richards in the play?

Thus our discussion might broaden to consider that, in damning the early Richard, Shakespeare has made it difficult for us to reconcile him with the later Richard, with whom we find ourselves in sympathy?

Does the characterization cohere?

The answer must take into account the subtlety of Shakespeare's portrayal of Richard:

—he is both a wastrel King and an attractive figure.

—he has an exquisite, sensitive nature, but he is egocentric.

—Richard's self-centredness is the consistent thread in his character.

—Thus Richard's life is a 'performance' and he is the 'star'.

—As an actor, he can play many parts: from King at Coventry to suffering, martyred royalty at his death. He can find 'the right lines' for any occasion.

—Like all great actors he can feel the emotions he expresses. We cannot call him a hypocrite: he lives his roles.

—And watching this performance, we are captivated.

(d) *Conclusion*: The question seems to imply that somehow the sympathetic Richard overwhelms our clear vision of his inadequacies. It would seem that the clarity with which the follies are exemplified cannot lead to our 'missing' them. But, in disagreeing with the contention explicit in the question, we lay ourselves open to the need to discuss the unity of the characterization. This we endeavoured to consider under Section C.

2 'Character is destiny.' Discuss with reference to the character of Richard.

3 Discuss the character and dramatic importance of John of Gaunt.

4 How important is the 'Garden Scene' to our understanding of the play as a whole?

5 Outline the significance of the Duke of York.

6 'A strong, but unattractive man.' How far do you agree with this estimate of Bolingbroke?

7 'The women could be omitted from *Richard II* without detraction from the main impact of the play as a whole.' Do you agree?

8 'There are no villains in the play.' Examine the truth, or otherwise, of this opinion and discuss the implications of your conclusion.

9 From the evidence of the play, can you glean any ideas which suggest that something precious is lost when Richard dies?

10 From the evidence of the play, can you decide what Shakespeare regarded as the essential attributes of a good king?

11 'Bolingbroke is not overtly ambitious.' Discuss.

12 What evidence in the play is there which indicates that Bolingbroke is a shrewd politician?

13 'Order is one of the main themes of the play.' Do you agree?

14 Discuss the importance of 'the past' in the play. By what means is it put before us?

15 What is the overall effect of the various prophetic utterances in the play?

16 'We sense, early in the play, that Richard is doomed, and throughout his fate seems inevitable.' Find evidence to reject or support this view.

17 'A very well-structured play.' Discuss.

18 'The imagery of the play contributes greatly to our appreciation of character and our understanding of the themes.' Discuss the truth of this statement with reference to *Richard II*.

19 Of what importance is the 'Divine Right of Kings' to our understanding of the play, and by what means does Shakespeare establish its significance?

20 'Shakespeare does not take sides.' Discuss with reference to the portrayal of Richard and Bolingbroke.

21 'England' is the real theme of *Richard II*. Discuss.

22 'In *Richard II* coldly efficient realism meets the irresponsible imagination of a poet, and breaks it.' Consider this view of the play.

Further reading

The Arden Shakespeare: Richard II, ed. Peter Ure (Methuen, 1956)

Casebook series: Richard II, ed. N. Brooke (Macmillan, 1973)

Studies in English Literature series: Richard II, ed. A. R. Humphreys (Arnold, 1967)

The Cease of Majesty, M. M. Reese (Arnold, 1961)

Angel with Horns, A. P. Rossiter (Longman, 1961)

The Elizabethan World Picture, E. M. W. Tillyard (Penguin, 1972)

Shakespeare's History Plays, E. M. W. Tillyard (Chatto and Windus, 1944)

Shakespeare from Richard II to Henry V, D. A. Traversi (Hollis and Carter, 1958)